URBAN LEGENDS

Strange Stories Behind Modern Myths

A.S. Mott

Ghost House Books

The Publisher: Ghost House Books
Distributed by Lone Pine Publishing
10145 – 81 Avenue   1808 – B Street NW, Suite 140
Edmonton, AB Canada   Auburn, WA USA
T6E 1W9   98001

Website: http://www.ghostbooks.net

National Library of Canada Cataloguing in Publication Data
Mott, A. S. (Allan S), 1975–
    Urban legends: strange stories behind modern myths / A.S.
    Mott; illustrated by Aaron Norell.
    ISBN 1-894877-41-1

    1. Urban folklore. I. Title.
GR78.M67 2004   398.2   C2004-900440-9

Editorial Director: Nancy Foulds
Production Manager: Gene Longson
Cover Design: Gerry Dotto
Layout & Production: Chia-Jung Chang
Illustrations: Aaron Norrell

We acknowledge the financial support of the Government of Canada through the Book Publishing Industry Development Program (BPIDP) for our publishing activities.

PC: P5

To Chris and Tonikka,
your legends will live on.

CONTENTS

Acknowledgments

In the acknowledgments to my last book, *Fireside Ghost Stories*, I left the impression that my editor, Shelagh Kubish, was a stern taskmaster whose harsh words frequently brought me to tears. Let me clear the record here by stating that that was just a joke and that she is, as well as being a highly adept and talented editor, a lovely person to boot. Having said that I do wish she would stop offering me the suspicious-looking fried food she keeps bringing in from home (I think this book has given her ideas)…

Let me also wipe away this empty page space by thanking all of the authors—of whom there are too many to mention by name—whose work in this field was invaluable in my putting this book together. I should then also thank all of the members of the credulous public, without whom none of us smarty-pants party-poopers would have anything to write about.

I also would like to thank the gregarious Aaron Norrell for his awesome illustrations; the kitty-hat wearing Chia-Jung Chang for her excellent design work and the mustachioed Gerry Dotto for his cool work on the cover.

And to wrap it all up, I would like to thank Nancy Foulds and Shane Kennedy. I am so grateful for their confidence in me that I'll do my best to make sure they don't eat the fried food Shelagh keeps unconvincingly insisting is plain old chicken.

Introduction

In the introduction to my second book, *Haunted Schools,* I told the story of my first genuine encounter with the power of an urban legend. It occurred during a party where a man insisted to me that he had seen the episode of *Sesame Street* in which the popular Muppet character Ernie had died of cancer. I knew for a fact that he hadn't, because I knew that no such episode existed and that the only reason people believed it had was that an unfounded rumor took hold a few weeks after Jim Henson's death. Even so, I could tell that the man sincerely believed he had seen the moment he described. What I didn't mention in my original telling of this story was that only a few months later I found myself once again awed by the power of urban myth, only this time it was my own brother who set the incident in motion.

At the time Chris was in his first year of university pursuing a degree in physical education, and he and I had started talking about some of our more bizarre exam experiences. It was then that he told me about something that he swore happened to a "friend of a friend"—a phrase that anyone who has studied urban legends recognizes as the first sign that they are about to hear another one.

According to my brother, this "friend of a friend" had taken a class in philosophy, and when he sat down to write the final exam he was shocked when he looked at the test in front of him. In the middle of the ominously white sheet of paper was the one question that had perplexed humankind since it had first thought to pursue the meaning of life. The test consisted of one word. It simply asked "why?" Stunned, the student looked around and watched as his fellow students looked at the test and started to furiously write down some kind of response that they hoped could satisfactorily answer a question so vast. Right then and there the student decided that he couldn't compete with the others and that there was no way he could come up with something that would even come close to what he figured the professor wanted, so with a sigh of failure he simply wrote "why not?" in his blue book and got up and handed it in. It was because of this that it came as a huge shock to him when he looked at his marks a few weeks later and discovered that not only did he pass, but he was the only person in the class who had gotten an A. In the end his simple two-word answer had been exactly what the professor had been looking for.

Even though I had never heard this story before, I immediately recognized it as an obvious urban legend, and I told Chris as much. He defended the story at first, but— unlike the man at the party—he relented when I explained to him why I thought the story was too fantastic to be believed. The first reason was that I myself had taken a philosophy class and found it to be quite hard. I knew how much was demanded from students in these classes, and I highly doubted that answering "why not?" on any question would result in anything more than a hard F. It also occurred to me that if such an incident had ever actually happened, the resulting furor would have made the national news. The other students who took the test would have vehemently protested the results, to the degree that lawyers would have been called and the courts would have gotten involved. Plus, if the story had actually happened there would be no way that a professor would give an A for "why not?" when the much better and more concise answer would have been "because!"

A few days later I found myself on an Internet newsgroup in which former university students were discussing the weirdest rumors they had ever heard about their schools, and I joined in by telling the above story. I made sure to state directly that I thought the story was fun to tell but wasn't true, so it came as some surprise to me when—within a period of a few hours—I received three emails from people who insisted that not only was the story true, but that it had happened to friends of theirs. Now since these three people didn't go to the same schools and did not even live in the same countries, I highly doubted they were talking about the same person. Despite my still-recent *Sesame Street* discussion, I was shocked by this response. For the most part the people who posted on that newsgroup were bright, skeptical people who I believed to be hard to fool, so those emails strongly reinforced to me the power of a seductive and prejudice-affirming urban legend.

When I started telling people I was working on this book, many asked me where I thought these stories came from and why they are so popular. For the first question I always reminded them of that game that we all played in elementary school where all the students sat in a circle and the teacher whispered a phrase into the ear of one student, who was then supposed to whisper it to the student sitting next to him or her. The phrase would travel around the circle until it came back to the teacher who would then repeat what she had just been told. Almost inevitably, the phrase she repeated bore little relation to what she had originally said. This, in a nutshell, is how urban legends happen. In the beginning someone makes a joke, tells a deliberately absurd story, misreports a true story or just tells the truth, and then the people they are talking to tell other people. As the story moves from person to person the facts change and often it gets more absurd, because the more absurd a story is, the bigger reaction it will get. It used to take years and even decades for this phenomenon to occur, but in this high speed digital age an unverified rumor can become a famous urban legend within a couple of weeks, if not days.

To answer the second question I always just shrugged and said "people believe them because they *want* to believe them." People want to believe that Chinese restaurants use cat meat because it confirms their prejudices against other cultures and justifies their reluctance to try new things. People want to believe that gang members are hiding under their cars to slash their ankles because it confirms their paranoia and their fear of the outside world. People want to believe that all it takes is a glib two-word essay answer to ace a difficult university course because it's reassuring to believe that good things can come easily.

Because of this underlying fact, studying urban legends is a surprisingly positive experience. When these stories are disproved, people are forced to conclude that the world isn't anywhere as cruel or dangerous or random as they imagine. Incidents that—according to urban legend—supposedly happen every day turn out to have never happened at all or—at the very worst—to have happened once or twice in ways that were nowhere near as dramatic as we had been led to believe. Chinese food is 100 percent feline free, no one is going to slash your ankles and the only honest way you're going to pass that test is if you study for it. I hope that after you read this book you feel safer than you did before you started it. After all, if these stories aren't true, then there is a good chance that many more of the frightening stories you see and hear are just as fictional.

As one final note, I just want to add that I tried to write a book that was in the best of taste and that the grand majority would find completely inoffensive, but I decided that my publishers would have difficulty selling a book that was only 20 pages long. Urban legends are often gross and crude and deal with subjects you wouldn't want to discuss with your grandmother, and while I've attempted to write about them with as much decorum as is humanly possible, there are going to be moments in the following pages where no amount of good taste or careful euphemism will make up for the vulgarity of a story's details. Although I suspect that those moments are going to be the ones people enjoy the most and relate to all their friends, I apologize in advance to those of you who feel differently with the reminder that I *did* warn you.

— A.S. Mott

1
Eat, Drink and Be Wary

*F*ew personality quirks are as telling as a person's eating habits. If you want to really get to know someone, the best place to meet him or her is at a restaurant. The type of food they order, and how they eat it, almost invariably supplies you with valuable insights into their personality. A person you thought was shy and reserved can give evidence of a daring soul by ordering the nuclear hot chicken wings instead of the mild. On the other hand, a seemingly loud and boisterous person can be proved to be all talk and no show by complaining about how strange and different all the dishes on the menu look. And when they order the blandest dish possible, you know that despite their bravado they're really frightened inside.

Knowing that our eating habits say so much about who we are, it comes as no surprise that there are so many urban legends about the subject. The level of revulsion you experience reading these eight food-related stories will say a lot about whether you are someone who considers eating an adventure to be enjoyed or a chore to be tolerated. If, after reading them, you feel queasy and in need of an antacid, chances are you are in the latter category. If, instead, you feel ready for a snack, then it is likely you belong in the former.

Either way, bon appétit, and remember to brush your teeth when you're done.

The Secret Sauce

One of the jobs I held before I became a writer was as a line cook at a Greek restaurant. It was there that I learned to dislike people who insisted on asking for changes or substitutions for their meals. While I sympathized and understood that many of them had allergies or a natural aversion to a particular vegetable, that sympathy wasn't enough for me not to curse them as I tried to pick out the green peppers from a Greek salad. Because of this experience, I take a certain amount of pleasure in the following urban legend about a young woman who asked for no mayonnaise on her chicken burger and got something much much worse.

According to the legend, the woman was incredibly health conscious and went into the fast food restaurant (the name of which changes from telling to telling, with virtually every major chain having been implicated) only because she was starving and there was nowhere else to eat for miles. She scanned the restaurant's illuminated menu and concluded that the only item she would consider eating was the chicken burger. When she got to the till she asked the glum-looking teenager what was on the chicken burger and she was told lettuce, tomato and mayonnaise.

"Okay," the woman decided, "give me one, but with NO mayo. Okay?"

The teen nodded and repeated the woman's order.

"One chicken burger."

"With NO mayo," the woman repeated.

"Yeah, whatever, no mayo."

Three minutes later the teen handed the woman her tray with her chicken burger on it and she went to sit down and eat

it. She lifted it out of its packaging and took a big juicy bite. She could tell by just that one taste that there was mayonnaise on her burger. Annoyed, she stood up and walked over to the counter, where she impatiently slammed down her tray.

"You put mayo on this," she told the teenager behind the counter. "Are you stupid or something? I told you two times that I didn't want any mayonnaise."

The teenager protested that no one had put any mayo on her burger.

The woman sneered and opened up the burger to show the kid exactly where the mayonnaise was.

"See!" she said, pointing.

The teenager looked down at the burger.

"That don't look like mayo to me."

The woman looked down at the burger. There in the middle of the meat was a large and disgusting growth that looked like a tumor. She nearly threw up right there when she saw that she had taken a bite out of it, and that from the opening she created oozed a thick stream of yellow pus.

* * *

As gross as this story is, take comfort in the knowledge that it never could have happened. The meat used by fast food restaurants for chicken burgers has been ground up and processed, making the appearance of a tumor impossible. There is also the fact that in the story the growth is invariably described as a tumor, which is a hard substance that does not contain any sort of disgusting liquid. While biting into a chicken burger from a fast food restaurant may be dangerous for your waistline, you have no reason to fear that you may bite into something disturbingly squishy.

The Care Package

Several urban legends deal with the subject of cultural misunderstandings. One good example tells of residents in an unnamed African country reacting with horror upon seeing jars of American baby food for the first time. According to the legend, the naïve foreigners mistakenly assume that the jars contain food made *from* babies rather than *for* babies. Stories like this are usually told to demean and belittle foreigners, highlighting their supposed ignorance and lack of sophistication. Of these stories the oldest and most frequently told is that of the foreign family who are slightly puzzled by a care package from their relatives in the New World.

Usually the family is described as being from a rural area in one of the lesser-known eastern European countries. When the rest of their family decided to make the move to America, they chose to remain at home and live a more simple life. Their relatives in America ended up flourishing and felt obligated to share their good fortune with their European relations, so they frequently sent care packages to the old country. The contents of these packages varied and often included strange delicacies that the rural family had never seen before. They enjoyed trying these exotic foods, and they looked forward to the arrival of the large boxes that always came wrapped in brown paper and twine.

This was why it didn't strike them as odd when one of these packages was delivered and proved to contain only a small glass jar filled with gray powder. Over the years they had received many items that had come in powdered form, so, as they had before, they cooked the mixture in boiling water and ate it along with their supper. While over the years the family had liked some of the foods sent to them more than others, this was the first time they found the food to be inedible. They tried their best to choke it down but gave up and threw it away, wondering what in the world made their American relatives want to send it to them.

A few days later, when a letter arrived, the family discovered to their disgust that there was a reason the gray powder tasted so foul. The letter was from their aunt who wrote:

I'm so sorry. I meant to include a note with my package, but I've been so distracted lately after all that has happened. Before your Uncle Milos died, he told me that he wished that his ashes be sent back to the old country and spread around the farmland where he had spent so many happy days as a young boy. I want to thank you for helping me make this last wish of his come true, and I hope it wouldn't be too much trouble if you said a prayer while you scattered his remains.

Thank you,
Auntie Jana

* * *

Like the story about the horrified Africans, it takes a certain amount of prejudice to accept this urban legend as true. No matter how rural and ignorant a family was, they would still be able to determine that the jar contained ashes before they tried to eat it. Being rural and foreign is not the same thing as being stupid, and anyone could tell that the contents of the jar looked just like the ashes in their wood stove or fireplace. Even so, the story is still told, proving once again that if an urban legend confirms a person's prejudice, it will be believed no matter how absurd it is.

Alcohol's Hidden Danger

Anyone who has ever spent a high school health class watching a documentary about the dangers of alcohol can easily rattle off the various ill effects liquor can have on a person. Possible addiction, brain damage, insomnia, liver failure, broken blood vessels and hallucinations are only the tip of the iceberg, but despite these risks people continue to drink. You have to wonder, though, if they would keep chugging down their beers if they heard the stories about the one danger of alcohol that is seldom mentioned in polite discussions of the subject. Would they be so keen to order another round if they feared that the alcohol being served to them was once used to preserve a dead body?

Two different urban legends deal with the subject of liquor contaminated by a decaying corpse. The first involves a group of people who either purchased or came across an old, deserted house. While searching through the house they went into the basement and were surprised to discover a collection of heavy wooden barrels. By the smell in the air, they could tell that the barrels contained Jamaican rum, and almost immediately they set about taking advantage of their lucky discovery. Over the next six months they tapped the barrels and drank to their hearts' content. It was only when they got to the last barrel that their reverie was broken. The rum from this barrel tasted different. It was spicier and it burned their throats. All who drank it complained afterwards that they suffered the most vicious hangovers of their lives. Their stomachs rumbled and their brains grew fevered. Finally, someone decided to investigate the contents of the barrel and cut off its top. What he found made him feel even sicker than he had before. There in the barrel was the body of a middle-aged man who—it was later determined—was the former owner of the house.

The second story is one of the many legends that purport to describe the true story behind a corporate conspiracy. It almost always involves a foreign beer company whose workers are shocked to discover a dead body in the large vat whose contents they have just drained into bottles that are already on their way to being delivered. Rather than recall the contaminated brew and risk a public relations fiasco, the management decides to pay off the workers who discovered the body, making them sign non-disclosure forms that guarantee their silence. The beer is delivered to stores around the world and thousands of consumers unknowingly quench their thirst with a strangely bitter beer.

* * *

Unlike some of the other urban legends in this book, these two stories aren't so outrageous that a person would automatically dismiss them as nonsense, but it doesn't take that much insight to figure out that they are both completely fictional. While it may seem hard to disprove a story as anecdotal as the first, the fact that versions of it date back almost 800 years and come from countries all over the world firmly establishes it as folklore and not fact. And to believe the second story requires an unhealthy amount of cynicism. As with most conspiracy stories, it falls apart if even the smallest modicum of logic is applied. For if the conspiracy was as successful as described, then the story wouldn't exist, and if even one person involved in the coverup told someone, then the result would be an international news story and a series of very costly lawsuits against the beer company. So, if you are like the millions of others who enjoy the occasional tipple, you are better off worrying about finding a designated driver than the possibility that the bottle of beer you just polished off tasted a little too fleshy or that the wine you just drank had a little too much body.

That's How They Get It so Soft

There is something supremely satisfying about bubblegum when you're a kid. Whether it's the sugary rush of flavor that takes over your mouth when you first pop it in, the joy that comes from blowing it into big round bubbles or the illicit thrill that comes from chewing it behind your teacher's back when you know you don't have a piece for everyone in the class, there are few pleasures as sublime. It's hard to imagine a world where it did not exist, but there was a time when it didn't. At least not in the form we appreciate it today.

Before 1975, chewing flavorful bubblegum was not the simple chore it is these days. Back then gum came in four varieties. You had your soft sticks such as Juicy Fruit and your hard shells such as Chiclets and vending machine gumballs, all of which were useless for blowing bubbles. You also had those thin chalky strips that came with trading cards, which were inedible and only to be chewed on a dare, and you had your big hunks of hard gum like Bazooka Joe and Dubble Bubble that had to be chewed for hours before you could get a decent bubble out of them and by then they tasted like old erasers. Knowing this, the Life Saver Co. decided to market a new kind of gum that was as soft as Juicy Fruit but that had the bubble-blowing possibilities of Bazooka Joe. They hoped that kids would immediately embrace a product that allowed them to blow bubbles with it while it still had its flavor. They named the new product Bubble Yum, and it was an instant smash. In fact, it was so successful that they soon had to take the unusual step of cutting down on their advertising so they could put more money into producing more gum more quickly.

It didn't take long, though, for kids to start to wonder just how they got the gum so soft. During the spring of 1977, the Life Saver Co. noticed that sales of the new gum had started to fall in the New York City area. The executives were puzzled as to why sales were slumping in this one city while they soared throughout the rest of the country, so they sent out some representatives to research the matter. They were shocked to discover that kids in New York had stopped buying Bubble Yum because they were convinced that it contained spider eggs, legs and webs. Stories of children waking up at night with hundreds of little baby arachnids crawling out of their mouths were being told all across New York's school-yards, and thousands of kids stopped buying the gum out of fear of facing the same nasty fate.

* * *

As with many urban legends it was impossible to pinpoint where this one had started, but the most obvious explanation was that some kids were wondering aloud how they got the gum so soft and someone—who most likely just wanted to gross out the other kids—suggested that it was made out of spiders. It is likely that from something as simple as that this explanation snowballed across the city until it became an avalanche that threatened the Life Saver Co.'s finances. Faced with the possibility that this rumor would begin to spread, the company took the unusual step of taking out ads that insisted that their product was 100 percent spider free. They spent over $100,000 on this campaign and eventually got their sales in the city back to what they were before the urban legend had begun to spread.

Even so, the legend that Bubble Yum contains spider eggs or legs has never completely vanished. Over a quarter century later, in a city thousands of miles away from New York, three different people have asked me if I knew about the gum when they learned I was working on this book. This is good proof that no matter how long an urban legend exists, it never really loses its flavor.

How Do You Like Your Eggs?

As with several other stories in this chapter, people's tendency to believe this legend depends on their natural cynicism regarding the food and service in fast food restaurants. Even though most people eat at these places more than once or twice a week, there is a persistent and unwavering belief among the public that doing so is very risky, which is why so many people didn't question the story when it popped up in an email that began circulating throughout November 1998.

Unlike the majority of fast food urban legends, which are so generalized that they can be described as taking place at any of the many franchises that exist, this story always implicates a Mexican food chain. It was there, the email insisted, that a young woman—who is not named—bought a chicken soft taco because she was in a hurry to get home and needed a quick bite to eat. Later that night the woman noticed that her jaw felt tighter than usual and that it was slightly swollen. She didn't think anything of it when she went to bed, but the next morning she awoke to find that the swelling had become much worse. Understandably worried, she went to her doctor, who decided that it was most likely an allergic reaction to something she ate. He prescribed a cream and told her to rub it on her face until the swelling went down.

A week passed and it became clear that the cream wasn't working. The swelling was just getting worse, and it was becoming more and more difficult for her to open her mouth. She went back to her doctor, who ran some tests on her to find out what was wrong. For one of these tests a saliva sample was taken from the roof of her mouth and it was here that the doctor discovered the horrifying truth.

Hundreds of cockroach eggs were incubating in her saliva glands inside her mouth. In order to save the woman the doctor sent her to the hospital where several layers of her upper mouth were removed, a procedure that had to be done right away because the eggs were only a few days away from hatching. After the operation the woman and her doctor tried to figure out how the cockroach eggs could have gotten in her mouth, and they concluded that there must have been a pregnant roach in the taco she had ordered from Taco Bell. The woman immediately brought up a lawsuit against the company, which is still pending.

* * *

Here is another case of people assuming a story is true, even though it defies credibility. The main problem with the story is that a cockroach egg sac would be much too large to get into a person's saliva glands—which, by the way, are designed to push saliva out and not to let foreign objects in. Even if the woman had eaten a pregnant cockroach, the egg sac would have been chewed up like the rest of the bug, and anyone who has watched an episode of *Fear Factor* knows that eating a cockroach may be gross, but it isn't dangerous. The other problem with this story is the question of how the woman and the doctor conclude that the roach was in the taco and not in any of the other foods she must have eaten over the previous week or so. Plus the actions of the doctor in this story are so incompetent that it would seem that if the woman involved should sue anyone, he would be the one. In fact, the final note about the lawsuit proves to be the legend's greatest undoing, as it doesn't take that much effort to discover that no such lawsuit exists on any docket in the American legal system.

A Little Something Extra

If you were to ask most people what menudo is, they would probably tell you that it was a Latin boy group from the 1980s with the famous policy of kicking out its members once they turned 16. What they may not be aware of is that menudo is also a Mexican dish made from beef tripe (the inner lining of a cow's stomach). This leads to the question of which seems like the worse prospect, listening to menudo or eating it.

In January 1987, a California-based food manufacturer found sales of its canned menudo plummet when rumors began to spread that a human finger had been found in one of its cans. It all started in the home of two brothers who shared the house with their wives. On the second day of the New Year, the four sat down to dinner, which that night consisted of a serving of canned menudo. While they dished out their servings, Freddie noticed something strange on his plate. It almost looked like a finger. Stunned, he passed it around to the others, who were both shocked and disgusted by what they saw. It had to be a finger, Phillip pointed out, because there was a fingernail on the end of it.

They saved the finger and threw out the menudo and took their discovery to a hospital. In many reports of the story, the hospital was said to have confirmed that it was indeed a finger, but the truth was that the hospital merely told them to take it to the police, which they did. The police reported the find to food inspectors from the United States Department of Agriculture, who took it so they could study it. In the meantime a reporter caught wind of the story and interviewed one of the policemen involved. He told the reporter that he had seen the finger and that a hospital had examined it. The story ran on the evening news and was picked up by a famed radio personality who reported that menudo was being removed from shelves all across California, but the truth was that it had been removed only from the one store where the brothers had purchased their supposedly tainted can.

Immediately after this people understandably stopped buying menudo, despite the California company's firm insistence that there was no way that a human finger could have gotten into their product. All the workers at the plant where the menudo was canned wore wire mesh gloves that could not be cut through by knives, and there had been no report of a serious injury of any kind when the can would have been manufactured. Their assurance that they had done nothing wrong was eventually proved correct, when the food inspectors reported that what the brothers had found was not a finger, but instead a piece of connective tissue commonly found in tripe. But by then it was too late. The company saw its sales fall by over a million dollars that year, and for the years to come people would hesitate before buying food from the people who had served up the human finger.

With Nine Lives
You Get Eggroll

Many of the stories in this book are so logically flawed and absurd it doesn't take much to convince people that they never really happened. There are, however, some urban legends that are so universally accepted by people that trying to convince them that they aren't true is nearly impossible. The idea that Chinese restaurants save money on meat by serving cats, rats, dogs and other kinds of stray animals is just one of these legends. It's something people have heard so many times that they just assume it must be true, even though the only evidence of this practice occurring is purely anecdotal and likely to fall apart if you look at it closely.

On occasion a Chinese restaurant will be shut down for health code violations, but so are Italian, Greek, German and virtually all kinds of ethnic and non-ethnic restaurants, so why then do Asian restaurants get saddled with the cat meat stigma? The answer goes all the way back to the 19th century when Asian immigrants were feared and looked down upon. There are cases from as early as 1850 when Asian entrepreneurs saw their once-busy restaurants become vacant as the result of slanderous rumors about the kind of meat they used. These rumors inevitably came from their competitors or racist townsfolk who didn't like the idea of an Asian immigrant becoming too successful.

It didn't help that Chinese families were less likely to own animals as pets, and that dog and cat were acceptable menu items in some far-off rural areas of China. However, immigrants who opened Chinese food restaurants were smart enough to know that serving dog or cat in dishes wouldn't be acceptable in North America. They also knew that the money they would have saved in the short term would have been quickly lost if and when people caught wind of the practice, so only the traditionally acceptable meats were ever used.

But still to this day if you ask the average person if the practice occurs in their hometown, chances are they will say that it does. As proof they will recite some story a friend of theirs told them about a friend of a friend who was a health inspector and found evidence of cat being used at a place that was just closed down.

Another story that people tell usually involves a doctor or a veterinarian who goes to eat at a Chinese restaurant and finds a strange bone in his food. Curious, he takes it home to analyze it and discovers that it's a rat bone. In some versions the bone becomes lodged in a poor diner's throat, and it is the doctor who removes it who determines its icky origin.

A good sign, though, that people don't take this urban legend too seriously is that Chinese restaurants do still exist, which means that even if people believe it they are willing to take the risk for the chance to eat some delicious Szechwan beef or deep-fried wonton. Luckily they make up the majority and the poor people who refuse to go to Chinese restaurants because of their ignorance are the ones who truly miss out.

Finger-Licking Gross

Late one night a young woman is driving home from work and decides that she has to get something to eat right away and turns into the first open drive-through that she sees. It's a fried chicken restaurant, so she orders a three-piece dinner with coleslaw and fries. She gets her food and starts to drive home, but she's so hungry and the food smells so good she decides she can't wait and turns into a parking lot and starts to eat. The first piece of chicken tastes so wonderful she sighs with pleasure as she eats it. Still ravenous, she digs into the second one, which is just as good as the first. Feeling sated, she pauses before she grabs the last piece. She might not be able to finish it, and she hates to waste food, but it smells too good to pass up so she takes a big bite out of it. As she chews she finds that this piece tastes different from the first two, gamier and tougher to chew. In the dark the piece looks normal, but it feels heavier than the other two. Curious, the woman turns on the light in her car and starts to gag when she sees that she has just eaten a bite of battered and fried rat.

This is just one of the many versions out there of the urban legend about the person who accidentally eats a part of an animal we normally prefer not to deep-fry. In others the person (who is most often described as female) is so horrified by her discovery that she has a heart attack and dies, or becomes ill from some strange rodent virus. Almost every version tries to get around the question of how the person would not notice what they had in their hands before they started eating it by having the victim eating in a dark place.

Once again this is a story that depends on our cynicism to be believed. Our natural prejudice about the quality of fast

food service is what keeps us from questioning the story's many logical faults, one of which is why would someone serve a deep-fried rat? Since the chicken at these restaurants comes to their outlets pre-battered, it would require a deliberate act of malice for someone to include anything other than chicken. It wouldn't be hard for the police to find out who did it, and chances are the responsible party would face not only losing their job, but a civil lawsuit and possible criminal charges. This prank is not only criminal; it's criminally stupid.

Strangely enough, though, in November 2000, an incident similar to this one occurred. Unlike the often-told legend, this one happened at a popular hamburger franchise. The restaurant was test-marketing a new deep-fried chicken wings meal and sold one to a Virginian woman. Among the wings she found a piece that looked nothing like the others, and that—on closer inspection—turned out to be a chicken's head. Two days later she and her husband informed the media that they had hired a lawyer and planned to sue the restaurant, and although the case is still pending chances are they will come away disappointed. The problems with their case include the facts that a) no one actually ate the offending piece and b) the woman has posed for several media photographs with the fried chicken head, which makes her assertion that it caused her personal anguish very hard to argue. After all it couldn't have caused her too much stress if she can hold onto it and show it to reporters.

No one knows how the chicken head got in with the chicken wings, so the question remains if it was just an accident or a deliberate prank. But the truth is that it is hard to see what the big deal is. It may be a chicken head, but at least it's still just a part of the chicken. Compared to the urban legend involving the rat, this woman got off rather easily.

2
Naturally Dangerous

*E*ver since mankind started to think of itself as mankind it has had a dysfunctional relationship with its environment. Sometimes we have taken the upper hand in the relationship by decimating entire forests and punching huge holes in the ozone layer, but then nature has also gotten plenty of licks in too, giving us an ice age, erupting volcanoes and the occasional earthquake to let us now that it's still in the fight. What this means is that like any dysfunctional family, we both love and hate each other. Both parties are capable of inflicting incredible cruelty on each other, but also incredible kindness. It is thanks to this bipolar relationship that for every story about the great glories of nature and all of its wonders, there is another story about how it's out to get us.

The eight legends that follow all fit into the latter category. They all represent legends that insist that when nature isn't blessing us with sunshine, rainbows and the sweet scents of spring, it's enlisting spiders, plants, bears, reptiles and even cows to confuse, humiliate and—ultimately—kill us. Which isn't that far from the truth, but there's no reason we should take it so personally.

The Mexican Cactus

Quentin had been in Mexico on business for two weeks when he realized that the day he was due to come back home was his wife's 36th birthday. So, after his last meeting was over, he ran over to a large marketplace and searched in vain for a decent gift. The problem was that Patricia wasn't the type of person who was impressed by the rustic wares of a foreign land. Her tastes ran towards the hip and modern, and he couldn't find anything that matched those two descriptions. He was about to give up when he spied a cactus sitting in a pot beside one of the stalls. It was tall, just over 2 feet, and it reminded him of something he had seen in a cartoon.

Looking at it, he tried to think of reasons she might like it. After a few seconds the best he could manage was that she loved plants and flowers, but she was always so busy she never had time to take care of them. Here, he justified, was a plant she didn't have to worry about. He then tried to think of reasons she might not like it, and there were quite a few of those, the most obvious being that *it was a cactus*. Still, despite the multitude of misgivings in his mind he bought the large cactus and brought it back to his hotel room, where he spent the last night of his stay trying to figure out how he was going to bring it on the plane.

Eventually he just called room service and asked them if they had any large boxes he could use. They brought some up, but they were all too small, so he cut them up and made a larger box out of them. He placed the cactus inside it and taped it up. The next morning he worried that they might not let it on the plane, but it got on and it also managed to make it through customs when he got home. Patricia was there to pick him up and he handed her the heavy box with a smile.

"Happy birthday," he said.

"What is it?" she asked him as she placed the box on the airport floor and began to open it.

"You'll never guess," he said, slightly nervously.

Her reaction when she saw it was muted, to say the least.

"It's a cactus," she said, her tone of voice suggesting that the joke was over and he had better offer up her real gift right away.

"Surprise!" He tried to muster up some enthusiasm.

"You got me a *cactus?*" she asked him as if he were crazy.

"I'm sorry," he apologized, "it was either that or a bottle of tequila, and I know how you're terrified of worms."

She looked at the cactus, which was still in the box.

"Well," she sighed, "at least I don't have to take care of it."

They took it home, and Patricia set it in a corner of their living room. The next day Quentin went to a jewelry store and got her something nice, even though, by then, she had actually come to like the odd gift. As busy as she was she attempted to care for it, and, as a result, the plant began to grow. After a year it had grown another 3 feet and had became a conversation piece in the room.

While she was watering it one day, she noticed an odd sound coming from the plant. It was a strange hum, one she had never heard before. She called out to Quentin, who was in the kitchen, and he came over and admitted that he heard the sound as well.

"What do you think it could be?" she asked him.

"I don't know," he said, shrugging. "I'm not a botanist."

"But isn't that weird? Cactus plants don't make sounds."

"Not that I'm aware of."

As they debated what was happening, the hum grew louder and louder. They stopped speaking as the cactus began to vibrate.

"Watch out!" Quentin warned Patricia. A 5-foot cactus could be quite deadly if it fell on you.

"What's going on?" she asked as they backed away.

Quentin didn't answer her, for at that moment a furry leg broke out of the top of the cactus. It was followed by another and another and many more after that.

Patricia almost fainted at the sight of the large hairy tarantula that emerged from her cactus. But somehow she managed to stay alert, which wasn't necessarily a good thing considering that that first tarantula was not alone. Spider after spider began to pour out of the top of the cactus. There were too many to count.

Patricia and Quentin screamed and ran out of the house. The authorities were called, and the sudden infestation was taken care of. The couple lived in a hotel while the house was fumigated and the last of the furry spiders was terminated. The experience, however, proved so traumatic for Patricia that when they were finally able to return to their home, she refused. So they sold the house to someone who didn't mind its history, and they bought a brand new one. Patricia didn't allow anyone to bring any plants or flowers to the house-warming party.

* * *

A truly international legend that has circulated through-out the world, the story of the infested cactus is one that comes in many different flavors. The tale told above is tame compared to some of the others. In one gruesome version, the spiders escape from the cactus late at night, when the couple is asleep. These poor people awaken to discover themselves covered by hundreds of deadly spiders, and though they survive, the young woman's lips are so damaged by the bites she receives that she has to have them amputated. How exactly a lip amputation is handled is a question I never want to have answered.

A much tamer version of the story has the couple avoiding the spiders completely. When the cactus starts acting strange, they call an expert—exactly what kind of expert differs from version to version—who warns them to get out of the house right away, thus sparing them the horror of the situation. In another version, the couple is spared the infestation of spiders but is forced to deal with scorpions instead. Despite all these differences, the versions of the story have one thing in common: they are all urban legends.

While there have been cases of spiders and scorpions creeping across the border by hiding in boxes of fruits and vegetables, no one has ever brought them over by purchasing a cactus. Tarantulas do not make a habit of living inside plants, preferring instead to live in underground burrows. A spider may spin a web and lay eggs on a cactus, but not inside one. Scorpions, on the other hand, might be found inside a cactus, but their reproductive abilities would not allow for an infestation such as this to occur. Scorpions do not lay eggs; instead they are born alive from their mother, whose pregnancy can last as long as 18 months. Not only would the number born be insufficient to cause the infestation described, but the babies would take so long to grow that a decade could pass before they became as big as the stories insist they are.

This legend is not the only one that deals with what can come from buying gifts south of the border. Another famous one involves a couple buying what they think is a small Chihuahua, only to discover when they get it home that it is really a large rat. One could formulate a theory about how these legends are indicative of a fear of the foreign, but most likely they are remembered more because of people's natural aversion to spiders, scorpions and small yappy dogs.

The Dangers of Plummeting Livestock

Over the 20 or so years Nobuo Ozu had served as the captain on various trawlers on the Sea of Japan, he had witnessed many strange events, some so bizarre he never bothered to share them with anyone else. But what had happened that Tuesday was so incredible that he and his crew actually doubted their own eyes when it happened.

It had been a clear morning and the sea had been calm. It was going to be a good day to fish, and the men were full of good cheer as they started to get to work. They laughed and told jokes as they lowered their nets, and they made bets about what their total tally for the day was going to be.

Their reverie was broken when, from out of the sky, they heard what could only be described as a tremendous mooing. They looked up and were amazed to see that a large dairy cow was plummeting towards them.

"Get down!" Nobuo ordered his crew.

Everyone scattered for safety as the terrified farm animal crashed into the middle of the boat. The impact was so heavy that the poor creature broke through the ship's deck all the way to its bottom. Water began to gush up from the newly formed cavity. Nobuo ordered his men to abandon ship, and they ran to get to the lifeboats before the trawler sank. Within two minutes they were all safely floating away from the sinking wreckage, each with a dazed expression on his face.

They floated on the waves of the sea for a day and a half before someone noticed they were missing and a ship was sent

out to look for them. They were cold and hungry when they were found, and when they were asked what had happened they remained oddly silent.

When they got back to the harbor, the authorities were waiting for them. The boat was owned by a private corporation, and it intended to press charges against whoever was responsible for the accident. The police interrogated the crew and the captain separately, but the seamen refused to say anything. Finally, knowing how strange it was going to sound, Nobuo broke his silence and explained what had happened that morning. His explanation was quickly met with incredulity.

"Are you telling us," asked the lead investigator, "that the boat was sunk by a cow that fell out of the sky?"

"Yes," insisted Nobuo.

"Do you think we're stupid?" asked the investigator's partner.

"I don't think I've known you long enough to make that judgment," answered Nobuo.

The investigators then confronted the crewmen with their captain's version of events, and they were shocked when the men confirmed Nobuo's story.

"What do you think?" the lead investigator asked his partner.

"They spent a long time out there on the ocean," his partner answered him, "they could have easily concocted the story after the ship sank."

"But why would they agree to tell *that* story? There must have been a better one they could have made up."

His partner shrugged.

"Maybe they're just stupid?" he guessed.

"Or maybe they figured that if they created a tale as unbelievable as this one then it would seem so strange that we would have no choice but to believe it—"

"—While we might question a more logical version of events."

"Crafty."

"But not crafty enough."

The investigators brought their findings to a judge who ordered that Nobuo and his men be sent to jail until they confessed what really happened that morning. The fishermen protested that they already had, but no one would believe them.

Nobuo and his men sat in their cells and despaired that they might never get out. They had told the truth and were imprisoned for it. After two weeks, Nobuo had decided that he owed it to his crew to go down with his ship, so he began to formulate a more plausible version of events in which he was responsible for the accident. He would then most likely be charged for the crime, but at least his men would be freed.

But before he was able to make this sacrifice, a guard came and told him to gather his things.

"They're letting you go," he told Nobuo.

Nobuo and his men were taken from the prison and were gathered together in a room with the sheepish-looking investigators.

"Your story checks out," the lead investigator reluctantly admitted. "It turns out your story made the international news services, where it got to the crew of a Russian Air Force cargo plane. When they heard that you were in jail they confessed to their superiors that they had stolen a cow off a Siberian airfield and had it in their hold while they were flying over the Sea of Japan. Apparently the animal went crazy and started to rampage inside the hold, and the crew had no choice but to jettison it at 30,000 feet."

"So you guys are in the clear," his partner confirmed.

Because he and his crew were not responsible for what happened, the company they worked for allowed them to keep their jobs and they were transferred to another trawler. And although they seldom talked about what had happened that morning, they always kept an eye towards the sky above them.

* * *

Since this story first appeared around the mid-1960s, the nationalities of those involved has varied somewhat, but these days the story almost inevitably involves a Russian airplane and a Japanese fishing trawler. Whatever countries the participants come from, the story is still a clear example of an urban legend that most likely started out as a joke. All it takes, in cases such as this, is a few people who confuse the obviously apocryphal anecdote as a true story, and within a few years it is being told not as a joke but as something that really happened. The obviously absurd nature of the story actually works in its favor here, as people are very often willing to accept a more outlandish story over a more logical one. If they didn't, books like this would not exist.

The Living Gun Rack

Virgil loved to hunt. Ever since his father had first taken him out to shoot deer when he was 13, he always counted the days to the start of the season. He loved being outdoors, becoming a part of nature. He loved the smell of the forest and its quiet symphony of sounds. But most of all he loved the thrill of the hunt, the glory of the kill. He could think of no better feeling than the power that surged through him whenever he pulled the trigger of his rifle and the shot rang out and his prey fell to the ground.

There was only one thing about hunting that came close to dampening his enthusiasm about it, and that was the fact that he wasn't very good at it. As much as he loved that surge of power, he had experienced it only five times in the 30 years he had been hunting. And of the five deer he had managed to kill over the years, none were the kind that people had mounted on their walls. Virgil's one dream in life, his only real goal, was to shoot a perfect four point buck and have its head mounted on his wall as proof of his prowess in the wild. But for that dream to come true, Virgil would have to depend on a miracle occurring.

But, then, sometimes, miracles do happen.

It was a cool Sunday morning, the day his license was due to end for the year. Despite having gone without a kill for six years in a row, he was still optimistic that he would get that buck that haunted his dreams. After a quick breakfast of bacon and scrambled eggs, he put on his hunting cap and vest and grabbed his rifle and started to make his way out into the forest. It had rained the night before and everything was still damp, and his boots made unfortunate sloshing sounds as he walked. He swore quietly under his breath, knowing that the sound would likely scare off any animals within earshot.

He tried to walk as slowly as he could, but his boots still made the same loud sound. Finally, he decided to just stop and hide for a while behind some foliage, with the hope that some stray creature would be kind enough to walk right between the crosshairs of his rifle.

He sat there as quietly as he could for three hours and saw not a single animal to justify his patience. He was just about to give up when finally the miracle he had been waiting for all his life happened at last. From behind a tree out stepped a true king of the forest. It was a genuine four point buck with the most impressive rack of antlers Virgil had ever seen. Tears came to his eyes as he thought about how good the animal's head would look above his fireplace. For the rest of his life he would be able to tell the story about how he had tracked and killed the most impressive specimen the forest had to offer. It would be the crowning achievement of his life.

His heart raced as he silently lifted up his rifle and aimed it at the deer. He was so nervous he was afraid that his shaking would affect his shot, so he took a moment to calm down before he closed his eyes and squeezed the trigger. He heard the sound of exploding gunpowder and he opened his eyes to see if his bullet had met its mark. He screamed with joy when he saw the huge buck on the ground. He then ran out from behind the foliage towards his fallen quarry. It was even more beautiful than he had dreamed. He knew then that every disappointing year he had spent out in the forest with nothing to show for it had been more than worth it.

He needed a picture. He had to document this moment on film. It could conceivably be the last good thing that ever happened to him, and he needed concrete evidence that it had occurred. Anyone could buy an impressively mounted deer head, but with a picture he could prove that he had gotten one the old-fashioned way. He rummaged through his pockets for the camera he always carried with him for just this purpose. He found it and set its timer to go off in one minute. He then placed it on a stump that was just a few feet away from the dead animal and walked over to the carcass and grabbed it by its antlers. He still had half a minute before the camera was to take the picture, and—with the antlers in his hands—he dreamed up the ultimate pose. With a smile of creativity he took his rifle and placed it on the buck's antlers, as if they were just like his gun rack at home. With this added touch now complete he beamed towards the camera, and counted down the seconds.

"Six...five...four...three...two—"

Before he could get to one, he was jerked off his feet by a shake of the buck's head. Before he knew what was happening, the large animal was back on its feet. The camera's flash went off just before the deer ran back to where it had come from, Virgil's gun still resting between its antlers.

Virgil never printed that roll of film. Even though the picture it contained would have made for an especially amusing anecdote, he chose to let it go forever undeveloped. For some reason, he just didn't think it was that funny.

* * *

The above story represents the North American take on a story that originated in Australia around the beginning of the 20th century. In this original version of the tale, a kangaroo was presented as the stunned animal that runs off with a person's belongings—a scenario that recently played itself out in the 2003 surprise hit film *Kangaroo Jack*. Unlike the American who is deliberately trying to kill the animal, the protagonist in the Aussie story accidentally hits the creature when it jumps out in front of him on the road. The motorist, who happens to be a tourist visiting the land Down Under for the first time, isn't too concerned about having killed the animal, as he instead decides to take the time to create a funny photograph for his friends at home. He takes off his jacket and hat and puts them on the kangaroo, only to have the seemingly dead creature come back to life and hop away with his jacket—along with his wallet, passport and car keys in the jacket's pockets.

There is, however, another stunned deer urban legend that is completely American in origin. Some people insist that the story is real, as it involves a recorded message that has circulated across the country thanks to bootleg tapes and the Internet, but the details of this recording are fuzzy and the message itself contains inconsistencies that lead many to believe it was a hoax. The credibility of the recording has been further damaged by the fact that several people have recreated it over the years, making it difficult to determine which one—if any—is the genuine article.

Known as the "Bambulance" recording, the tape consists of a call made to a police station by a drunken man in a uniquely dire situation. According to the man, whose words are slurred, he requires the aid of a "bambulance" because he received wounds from a frightened deer and ferocious canine. He explains that he was driving on the road when he hit the deer with the car. Assuming the animal was dead, and not one to waste good meat, the man stuffed the critter into the backseat of his car and started to drive home. While he was driving, the animal awoke and naturally panicked when it found itself in this alien environment. It started to thrash about in his backseat and bit the man on the shoulder. The man stopped the car at a phone booth and got out to call for help. When he stepped out of his car he drew the attention of a large and angry dog, which ran up to him and bit him on his leg. Doubly wounded, the man grabbed a knife and tire-iron from out of his truck and used them to keep the dog at bay. He then made it to the phone booth, where he placed the call that gets recorded. He can't tell the dispatcher how to find him, so during the phone call he is forced to get out of the phone booth and try to avoid the dog while he searches for recognizable landmarks and street signs.

Though the recording has many ardent defenders, most of the evidence points to its being a practical joke. But with so many different versions of the recording available, and so many theories about how it originated, it seems unlikely that the truth will be revealed any time soon.

Bad Hair Daze

At a school where the majority of the female population had followed the trend for massive and ornate hairdos, Sheri-Lou Roswell's was easily the most impressive. The 16 year old was usually only 4'11", but with her hair shellacked and hairsprayed towards the heavens, she became almost a foot taller. To look at this mightily impressive work of engineering was to wonder how her tiny little neck could carry the weight of it without snapping like a twig.

The truth was that if her entire coiffure had consisted of nothing but her own naturally red hair, she wouldn't have been able to wear it without suffering the torture of constant migraines and crippling back pain. Knowing this, the crafty young lady had constructed a device using wire and rubber bands that sat on top of her head. She then wove her hair through it, until the device was completely obscured. Thanks to this she was able to get her hair higher than anyone else's, using half as much of it. None of the girls could figure out how she did it. None of them knew that it was because her great tower of hair was hollow inside.

Occasionally other girls would try to outdo her and arrived at school grimacing from the pain, but the next day she would come in with her hair even higher, without a care in the world. Sheri-Lou had to deal with a large amount of jealousy from the other girls, which she ignored as gracefully as she could. She paid no attention to the rumors that her hair was secretly infested with roaches or spiders, and instead devoted her non-hair-related thoughts to Chuck Tussel, the school's star quarterback. As the other girls schemed of ways to bring her down a peg, she schemed of ways to seduce the dull-witted thrower into asking her to be his date for the prom.

Finally, her various tricks and schemes hit pay dirt, and the handsome lunkhead asked her to go with him. She played it cool and told him that she'd be happy to, with a charming smile plastered sweetly on her face. When he was gone she squealed with delight. Being his date virtually guaranteed that she would be made queen of the prom.

Word began to spread that she and Chuck were going to the prom together, which proved too much for one of her rivals to take. Joanie Harrington had the second highest hairdo at the school, but unlike Sheri-Lou's, hers was completely genuine. She carried her also-ran status as a badge of shame, and seeing her better becoming attached to the most popular boy around sent her clear over the brink. Like Sheri-Lou, she knew that going with Chuck to the prom ensured that the big-haired egotist would be crowned queen of the prom, and she decided that if that happened, then it would be a coronation no one would ever forget.

During the weeks leading up to the big night, Joanie tried to think of different ways she could humiliate her hated rival. She was doing exactly that one afternoon on the school's front lawn when she saw a large spider walk across the grass beside her. The lightbulb that flashed inside her mind grew so bright it exploded. She knew exactly what she was going to do. She was going to make the rumor that had plagued Sheri-Lou for the past two years a reality.

The problem was that she had no clue how to do it. As she tried to come up with a plan, she started to collect various insects and spiders using a pair of tongs and a glass jar. Soon she had enough to cause more than just an itchy scalp. But she had only two days before the prom and still had no idea how she was going to get the bugs into Sheri-Lou's hair. Finally she decided she would have to go to Sheri-Lou's house and spy on her to get an idea about how to get the job done.

She waited for nightfall before she left to find a spot where she could look into Sheri-Lou's bedroom window, hoping that her target wasn't so modest that she closed her curtains.

Luck was on her side that night. As it turned out, there was a tree beside Sheri-Lou's bedroom window that was very easy to climb, and the bedroom curtains were wide open. Wearing her older brother's blue jeans and an old sweater, Joanie shinnied up the tree and watched as Sheri-Lou walked into her room and closed the door behind her.

Like all the other girls at their school, Joanie had no idea about Sheri-Lou's secret method for incredibly high hair. This meant she also didn't know Sheri-Lou's other secret, which was that doing her hair was such a complicated task that she would go for weeks without doing anything to it. She didn't wash it or comb it or anything. She had a special pillow that she used to keep it from getting mussed up when she slept. It was only when she had to make it bigger or it simply became too messy that she went to the trouble of taking it apart and redoing it.

It was in near-perfect condition at the moment, so she had no reason to mess with it as she sat down in front of her bedroom mirror. But, as Joanie watched, Sheri-Lou scratched her head over and over again.

"Not again," she sighed to herself.

Sheri-Lou grabbed a strange tool from her table. It was long, and on one end was a trio of steel wires that came together to form a kind of claw. On the other end was a round metal button connected to a spring. When Sheri-Lou pushed the button forward, the spring pushed the wires out, causing them to open up. When she let go of the button, the wires went back and formed the claw. Joanie figured out that the tool was used to grab things with, but she had no idea what Sheri-Lou needed to grab.

As she watched, Sheri-Lou took the tool and worked it into her hairdo. She moved it around for a few seconds before she pulled it out. Joanie nearly fell out of the tree when she saw that, trapped in the grasp of the tool's claw, was a large squirming cockroach. She couldn't believe her eyes when she saw that Sheri-Lou wasn't finished. She went back in with the tool, and this time she took out a plump daddy-long-legs. She did this three more times before she was finished. Each bug she pulled out was bigger than the one that preceded it.

Joanie got down out of the tree, not knowing what to do. She had planned to take the rumor that Sheri-Lou's hair had bugs in it and make it true, but it actually *was* true, and now that she had seen it she knew no one else would really believe it. As a vicious spiteful rumor it was perfectly acceptable, but as a genuine reality it was just too horrible to believe.

As Joanie walked home she no longer wanted to get even with Sheri-Lou. She felt sorry for her. Yes, her rival had the biggest hairdo in the school, but it came at a price few people would be willing to pay. She decided it would be better to just let Sheri-Lou be prom queen without any trouble. She had earned it.

Joanie was standing with her friends when Chuck and Sheri-Lou walked into the gymnasium together. Chuck looked dreamy handsome in his tuxedo, and Sheri-Lou looked radiant in her long pink dress.

"There's old cockroach head," muttered Ginger, one of Joanie's friends.

"That's not nice," chided Joanie.

"What are you talking about?" asked Lindsey, another friend. "You're the one who's always talking about the bugs she has to have up there."

"Well, it was stupid of me to do that," Joanie insisted. "No one has bugs in their hair like that."

Her friends all looked at her, wondering if maybe aliens had kidnapped her and replaced her with a more polite robot version of herself.

"Stop looking at me like that," she ordered them. "I just realized that being catty never did anyone any good, that's all."

Her friends kept eyeing Joanie suspiciously, so she sighed and walked away from them and went to get some more punch. She was ladling some into her glass when the principal took the stage and made an announcement over the sound system. It was time, he informed everybody, to coronate the king and queen of the prom.

Everyone gathered in front of the stage as he opened the envelope that contained the names of the two lucky kids. The whole process was somewhat anticlimactic since everyone already knew who had won. That was why the cheers and applause were somewhat strained when Chuck's and Sheri-Lou's names were announced.

The honored couple walked onto the stage to receive their crowns. Sheri-Lou was halfway up the stairs when she suddenly cried out in pain and collapsed down the steps. Chuck and the school's principal rushed to her and were stunned to discover that she wasn't breathing. An ambulance was called, but it was too late. By the time the paramedics had arrived, it was obvious that Sheri-Lou was dead.

In the days that followed all the students who had been there tried their best to figure out what had happened that night. Joanie was with her friends when they started talking about all the different rumors they had heard about the cause of Sheri-Lou's shocking demise. They talked about heart attacks and aneurysms before Ginger told them something she had heard from a friend of her father's, whose cousin was the county medical examiner.

"He told me that she had been poisoned."

"How?" asked Joanie.

"You're not going to believe it," Ginger teased.

"Try us," ordered Mindy.

"From a spider bite. Apparently, and I'm not making this up, she *really* did have bugs in her hair, and one of them was a black widow spider."

All the other girls, except Joanie, groaned.

"That's just stupid," frowned Lindsey.

"Yeah," agreed Vivian, "that couldn't have happened."

"The bugs in the hair thing was just a joke," Mindy chimed in.

Ginger protested that what she had heard was true, but they all refused to believe her. Except for Joanie. She alone knew that the story had to be true.

* * *

It doesn't take too much research to guess when this particular urban legend first became popular. The hairstyles described in it are so obviously a fixture of the '50s and early '60s, along with poodle skirts and hula hoops. In more modern versions of the story, the central character is usually a man with dreadlocks rather than a woman with a large bouffant or beehive. Whatever the period, the story is another example, like the legend about Maria Callas, of a morality tale about the high price vanity can have on a person's well-being.

This legend is referenced several times in the John Waters' film *Hairspray*—which has since become a hit Broadway musical. In the over-the-top comedy, a teenager named Tracy Turnblad is sent to her school's remedial class because her huge bouffant blocks her fellow students' view of the blackboard. Tracy becomes a dancer on a popular afternoon rock and roll show, where her bubbly charm instantly makes her a popular sensation. Out of jealousy another popular dancer, named Amber Von Tussle, insists that she has seen a cockroach in Tracy's hair. By the film's end, Tracy has renounced her bouffant days by ironing her hair straight and she takes ownership of Amber's insults by creating a dance called "The Bug," which she introduces while wearing a dress covered with pictures of cockroaches. Amber, meanwhile, does Sheri-Lou one better by wearing a similarly complex wire construction on her head, only it contains a bomb—meant to go off if she isn't voted queen of the carnival—instead of the standard creepy crawlies.

As strange as it sounds, there may in fact be one instance where an incident similar to Sheri-Lou's actually occurred. "May" is the operative word, because even though the story has appeared in several international news reports, it has never been completely verified. According to the reports a young woman in the country of Yemen—where bigamy isn't uncommon—died after the jealous first wife of her husband-to-be placed a live scorpion inside her ornate wedding wig.

The 20 year old was said to have complained about several painful stings, but the hairdresser who put the wig on her assured her that she was just feeling pinches from the hairpins needed to keep the wig on. The bride collapsed soon after, having been stung 24 times by the scorpion.

Whether this is a true story or another urban legend, it stills serves as good proof of that old moral: never believe a hairdresser who tells you nothing's wrong.

A Photo Opportunity

William Calloway had been a park ranger for over 25 years. A strong, silent man who believed in the virtue of action over words, he was not the type to give into his emotions. One legendary story about him detailed the time he got his left leg snared in an illegal animal trap left by a poacher. The trap's heavy jaws had broken his leg, but somehow he found the strength to open the trap and get back to his cabin, 5 miles away, where he reset the bone himself before calling for a doctor. Whenever asked about the incident, he would just shrug and say that he didn't know what the fuss was all about. He had just done what he had to do to survive.

It was obvious then that he was not a man known for his sentiment. But there was one incident that had happened years before that still brought tears to his eyes whenever he thought about it. And though he was uncomfortable becoming so vulnerable in front of other people, he often told the story to the tourists who came to visit the park. He hoped that by seeing his tears they would know that he was serious when he told them that sometimes you just have to let a photo opportunity go by.

The Bushes were a young couple, both in their late 20s, when they came to spend a week camping in the forest. Neither of them had ever left the city before, but they wanted their young son, Omri, to have all the experiences that they hadn't. As Omri was only five years old, it wasn't clear how much he appreciated his parents' discomfort in the wild, but he enjoyed running around the large space and trying to climb the seemingly infinite number of trees. Their week was coming to a close, and the one thing they felt they had missed was a chance for Omri to share a moment with an animal. They had hoped to get a picture of him with some benign forest creature, knowing it would be a reminder of a time Omri would cherish for the rest of his life.

Unfortunately, the opportunity never arose, and they had given up on the idea as they were packing up to go. Jorge was folding up the tent, and Noelle was packing the other supplies when they heard their son behind them.

"Mom! Dad!" he shouted excitedly. "Look!"

They turned around and saw a smallish black bear, bigger than a cub, but smaller than a full-grown adult.

"Get the camera," Jorge whispered to his wife.

Quickly, Noelle unpacked the box she had just filled and pulled out their camera. She handed it to her husband. He took it and walked carefully towards his son and the bear.

"Omri," he whispered, "stay right there and hold out your hand."

His young son nodded at this and did as he was told. He held out his hand to the bear, but the animal didn't seem to be that interested in it. It looked around for a moment before it decided to turn back around.

"You're losing him!" Noelle hissed to her husband under her breath.

"What can I do?" he shrugged.

Noelle looked down among the goods she was packing up and had an idea. She grabbed some honey, spread it on a piece of bread and handed to Jorge.

"Give this to Omri," she told him, "bears like honey."

Jorge nodded and handed the bread to their son, who squealed with delight and licked some of the honey. The sweet scent of the liquid wafted through the air, causing the young bear to stop and look around.

"That's it," Jorge whispered as the bear started to turn around and head back towards their son.

At this point during the telling Ranger Calloway always broke down.

"The bear was young," he would tell the tourists listening to his tale," but that didn't mean he wasn't strong. He wanted that honey and he got it. It happened so fast that there was nothing the couple could do to stop it. That animal attacked their son and killed him right in front of their eyes. So let that be a warning to you. The animals in this forest are wild. They aren't like the cute domesticated animals you see on TV and in the movies. I don't care what you saw on *Gentle Ben* or *Grizzly Adams*, if you see a bear, don't let your children anywhere near it."

Some of those who heard this story assumed that the ranger had made it up just to scare them. They couldn't believe that anyone would be stupid enough to hand honey to a child to entice a bear for a photograph, but what they didn't know was that not only did Ranger Calloway not make up the story, but he had changed it so it was more believable. He knew that no one would believe what had really happened—that the couple had been so desperate for a good photograph that they had smeared honey on their son's face and told him to stand there until a bear happened by.

* * *

Even though this particular urban legend is as fictional as the others that appear in this chapter, the truth of its message should not be dismissed. Over the years many people who have spent their lives watching fantasies concocted by Hollywood harbor the illusion that the animals in the wild are kind and tame creatures. This is far from the truth. Every year hundreds of people are either killed or mauled because they failed to appreciate that an animal in the wild is by definition a wild animal, capable of sudden and devastating acts of violence.

As recently as October 9, 2003, a man named Timothy Treadwell and his girlfriend, Amie Huguenard, were both killed by a bear in the Alaskan wilderness. What made their deaths particularly newsworthy was that not only was the attack recorded on videotape, but also the victims were not ignorant tourists who found themselves in a situation they couldn't handle. Instead, Treadwell was a noted wildlife author who had cowritten a book entitled *Among Grizzlies: Living with Wild Bears in Alaska.* That he died by a bear mauling serves as proof of the legend's moral. If a man who had spent years studying bears, and who had even written a book about living with them, can be caught off guard and killed by one, what chance does an average person have when confronted by one?

That being said, it is asking a lot to expect people to believe that two people would be stupid enough to smear honey on a child's face to entice a bear into a photograph. True, acts of stupidity of this magnitude are not unheard of, but they are—thankfully—rarer than we might assume. There have been incidents where a parent's failure to appreciate the danger of a situation has resulted in the death and injury of their child, but never in the way described above.

Under the Seat

Cynthia smiled sweetly as her friends and the restaurant's wait staff sang "Happy Birthday" to her loudly enough for everyone in the building to know that she was another year older. Normally she would have felt uncomfortable and self-conscious about the attention, but during the previous few months she had splurged on a whole array of cosmetic operations and she looked and felt 10 years younger than her 37 years. Now she enjoyed the feeling of having every eye in the restaurant aimed in her direction. Not one of them would be able to correctly guess how old she really was.

She took a long sip from her glass of wine and took the tiniest bite from her slice of free birthday cake before she offered the rest of it to her friends, who gobbled it up without hesitation. It was then that it occurred to her that there was a way to guess her true age and that was by looking at the people sitting with her. She decided then and there that she had to make an effort to find new and younger-looking friends, as there was no point looking 27 if she was just going to spend her time with a bunch of 37 year olds. With this idle thought floating in her mind, she stood up and excused herself and walked to the women's washroom.

Like the restaurant itself, the ladies room was immaculate. Gleaming white tiles covered the floor and walls. A small settee was at the far end of the room beside a small table on which sat an exquisite bouquet of wild flowers. Cynthia noted that most people's living rooms weren't as nice as this bathroom. She was surprised to find that it was empty, having grown used to walking in on the private conversations some women insisted on having away from their husbands or boyfriends. She appreciated the silence her solitude allowed, punctuated as it was by the sound of her high heels clicking against the tile. She stole a glance at herself in the mirror, and took no small pleasure in what she saw, before she stepped into an empty stall.

The seat was cold, which she took as a good sign, meaning it had been awhile since someone else had used it last. She wasn't the type of person who was phobic about germs, but she did think about these things. As she sat there she heard the sound of the bathroom door opening and the chatter of two women gossiping happily.

"Did you see that woman they sang 'Happy Birthday' to?"

"I know, isn't that sad?"

"I mean, if you're going to get a facelift, don't get it so tight you can hardly blink your eyes."

"And those lips! She had so much collagen injected into them she looks like Mike Tyson punched her in the mouth."

Cynthia was stunned by what she was hearing. So stunned that she did not even notice the sharp and sudden pain that shot through her left buttock. What were these women talking about? Her doctor had done an excellent job on her facelift, and she didn't even get collagen injections. Her lips were naturally voluptuous. They were jealous, she decided. They were so envious about the way she looked that the only way for them to fight their own insecurities was to make catty remarks.

She waited for the women to leave before she left the stall and washed her hands. She took another look in the mirror to make sure her own eyes were not deceiving her, and— once again—its reflection assured her that she looked fantastic. She walked out of the washroom and back to her friends.

It was when she sat down in her chair that she first noticed the pain in her left buttock. Her best friend, Jackie, caught her grimacing.

"What's wrong, Cyn?" she asked her.

"I don't know. Just a weird pain."

"Have another glass of wine, that'll fix it."

Cynthia smiled and took her friend's advice and poured herself another glass of wine. She joined in on the table's conversation about the latest movies that were out and took long sips from her glass. As the minutes passed she began to feel slightly woozy. Her vision started to blur, and she started to feel unusually hot. Fearing she had drunk too much, she pushed away her half-full wine glass and tried to concentrate on what her friends were saying.

Once again Jackie noticed that her friend looked unwell.

"Are you okay, Cyn?"

Before she could answer, Cynthia felt a sudden flash of heat and was blinded by a bright white light. Consciousness ebbed out of her body and she fell forward, her head slamming against the table. Her friends jumped up and shouted for help, and an ambulance was called.

At the hospital the doctors determined that Cynthia had gone into a coma, but they had no idea why. They asked Jackie about everything she had noticed before Cynthia passed out, and taking a cue from her observation of the pain evident on her friend's face when she sat down, they examined her body. On her left buttock they found a small red bite mark. With this clue they performed a series of toxicity tests and determined that a poison was the cause of her coma, but they still needed to find out what had bitten her if they were to discover if there was an antidote.

They had no idea what to do next, but two days later another woman came into the hospital with the same condition. She also had the same bite mark as Cynthia did. Noting the possibility that such incidents may have happened before, they called all the local hospitals and found four other comatose women with similar bite marks. It didn't take them long to discover that all six women had fallen ill shortly after eating at the same restaurant.

Health inspectors were sent to determine what could be behind these illnesses. The restaurant was kept in immaculate condition, and it took a long time to find the source of the problem. While searching through the ladies washroom, one of the inspectors spotted a small spider crawling beside a toilet bowl. Moving slowly and cautiously, he crept towards the tiny arachnid and captured it in a small plastic vial. They took their find to an expert, who informed them that it was a species known as *Arachnis gluteus*.

"I'm not surprised you found it in a bathroom," the expert told them. "These guys love to lurk under toilet seats. What does surprise me is that you found it in a North America bathroom, as they are generally found only south of the equator. Luckily, there is an antidote to their venom, so the women who have been bitten have a good chance of getting better and returning to normal."

Using the expert's advice, the doctors were able to prepare the antidote and it was administered to all the women who were bitten. Of the six, five woke up a few days later and needed only a few weeks of rehabilitation before they were able to return home.

Cynthia was the only one who didn't wake up. The drugs she had been taking as part of her recuperation from her recent surgeries were still in her system, and they reacted badly when mixed with the antidote. Her coma became irreversible. She was spared the torment of 32 birthdays before she finally died at the age of 69.

* * *

A person doesn't need university courses in Latin in order to spot this story's obvious clue that indicates its status as an urban legend. Just take a look at the Latin name given to the story's venomous creepy crawly. It's *Arachnis gluteus*, or—translated into basic English—a butt spider.

Like many versions of this legend, no attempt is made to identify the source of this exotic spider. The expert notes that it is not a North American species, but he makes no guesses about where it could have come from. Other versions solve this by describing how the spider arrived in a box of vegetables that was delivered to the restaurant; either that or the locale of spider is changed from a restaurant's washroom to an airplane's.

Although it is rare, there have been cases of dangerous foreign spiders being found inside produce crates (ones containing grapes being the most common). As well, there are spiders that make a habit of living under toilet seats. Does this mean that you should take great care to inspect your commode every time you have need to use it? Of course not. The likelihood of your suffering the same fate as poor vain Cynthia is about the same as your winning a 100 million dollar lottery. Meaning it could happen, but in reality you'd do as well to be paranoid that a rampaging bull might gore you while you sit waiting in a doctor's office. Hey, if you're going to have unreasonable fears, they might as well be creative.

At the Outlet Store

Among her friends and family, Marjorie had a reputation for being frugal, though people seldom used such polite words when they talked about her. Cheapskate, miser and skinflint were the words they used most often. Marjorie did not understand what they were complaining about. She just understood the value of a dollar and she did her best to ensure that she always got the best deal she could. It didn't make any sense to her to go to a fancy store and spend hundreds of dollars on new things when there were so many thrift and outlet stores around where you get twice as much for half the price.

But like a lot of people who were so obsessed with saving money, there was no clear idea of what Marjorie was saving it for. She had no children, and she lived in the house she had grown up in. A combination of a large inheritance and some smart investments had made her quite wealthy, which meant her penny-pinching ways had nothing to do with a lack of funds. She could easily afford to wear the latest fashions, drive an expensive car, travel around the world and eat at the nicest restaurants, but instead she chose to wear second-hand and discount clothes, ride the bus, go nowhere and buy only the cheapest frozen dinners the supermarket had to offer.

Her attitude toward money wouldn't have been a problem if it didn't affect how she treated the people around her. Despite her wealth, she refused to give people birthday and Christmas gifts, considering them a horrible extravagance. And when she received gifts she would inevitably return them and pocket the cash (and heaven help the poor clerk who told her she needed a receipt). The only reason she gave money to charity was because her accountant had told her it was a nice tax write-off, but once she had given her annual allotment she refused to hand out a penny more, even though she could afford to give 10 times as much. But the worst side effect of her neurosis was that it made her paranoid and suspicious of everyone. Afraid that every person she met was out to rob her blind, she often became abusive and shrill. Once she even tried to get a grocery cashier fired for short-changing her by a nickel. When the manager refused, insisting that it was an honest mistake, she tried to get him fired as well. The owners of the store took the same stance as the manager, and from that point on she boycotted the supermarket, even though it was across the street from her house and the next closest store was 5 miles away.

It was unusually cold that fall. Marjorie knew this because the wind blew right through her autumn coat. It was almost two decades old and time had taken its toll on it. To her chagrin she finally admitted that it was time to replace it. In the same building across the street that held the supermarket where she refused to shop was a clothing store that was well stocked with a large variety of exactly the type of jacket she needed, but she considered their prices exorbitant. Instead she spent three hours on the bus to get to a large outlet store on the very edge of the city. There she found jackets that were almost as good for half the price. Normally when shopping, she would find what she needed, buy it and leave, not being the type to stay and browse, but—since she had spent so much time to get there—she decided to take a look and see if she could find any other bargains.

The already low prices at the store were even lower that day because of a half-off sale, which meant that it was

swarmed by a mass of similarly inclined bargain hunters. Not being a group renowned for their sense of decorum or friendliness, they pushed and shoved each other as they tried to find those fabled items that were of regular store quality but that had been sent to the outlet by accident. Marjorie fought along with the toughest of them, and she managed to grab some great and extraordinarily cheap finds. She even went so far as to grab a skirt directly out of the hands of one woman, and she coldly stared her down when she tried to protest.

She had found everything she felt she needed and was about to leave when she spotted out of the corner of her eye a blouse that she thought went well with her newly acquired skirt. She had to hip check a woman out of her way, and she had a triumphant smile on her face when she went to grab it. The smile faded when a sudden flash of pain jolted through her arm. She looked down and screamed loudly when she saw a smallish brown and green snake with its fangs sunk deeply into her arm. Somehow the small reptile had found its way into the blouse and when she lifted it up, it decided to defend its home.

Marjorie panicked and shook the snake off her arm. She stomped on it when it landed on the floor, but it was too late. The snake may have been small but its venom was strong. Just seconds after she had screamed and killed the snake— attracting the attention of everyone around her—she began to feel dizzy and nauseated. She collapsed to the ground and within minutes an ambulance was there to pick her up. Unfortunately it was too late. By the time she got to the hospital the paramedics had to write her up as dead on arrival.

Marjorie had never drafted a will, not wanting to ever contemplate other people getting their hands on her money, so her estate was divided up among her relatives. Had she still been alive to see it, she would have been scandalized by the way they spent her money. Some of them spent it on long vacations; some bought new cars and expensive electronic equipment. Others gave it to charity and one of her cousins even went so far as to spend the money on an expensive aquarium in which he kept an equally expensive exotic snake.

* * *

Unlike other similar legends about deadly animals killing people in the most mundane settings, this one makes no attempt to describe how the snake actually got into the store. Instead, almost every version of this legend focuses on the personality of the shopper, who is always described as a cheap woman. The effect this has on the story is to transform it from a tale warning about dangers that can pop at you from out of nowhere, into one about the horrible things that can happen to you if try to avoid paying retail. One has to wonder if maybe this means that the story was dreamed up by some upscale clothing company that wanted to steer people away from their lower-priced competitors.

In the autumn of 2003 it appeared that this legend had come true when a man claimed to have been bitten by a loose rattlesnake in a Texas branch of a well-known discount department store chain. The evidence, however, indicates that this was a case of a person being inspired to recreate an urban legend in the hopes of financial gain. The hospital the man was taken to has insisted that the man had not been bitten as he had claimed and has accused him of stealing its services. To add to the chain's claims that the incident was a hoax are the comments from the policeman at the scene who suggested that the diamondback snake—which the man insisted he had stomped to death after it bit him—looked to have been dead for a lot longer than the man's story would have allowed.

One of the benefits of faking an urban legend such as this one is that the story is so familiar. People who might otherwise doubt the man's claims may be inclined to accept them because they have heard about a similar incident, and despite the questionable nature of his story, it does match up with something that apparently happened someplace else some other time. The fact that no one knows when and where it was supposed to have happened seldom gets mentioned, as people frequently respond to things they remember without thinking about how they know them. For example if in tomorrow's newspapers there was a story about a person who claims to have found a human finger inside a can of food, people will instantly recall the menudo incident in California and assume the story is true, even though in that first case the strange object turned out not to be a finger.

But just because a lot of people will believe the person who pulled off the hoax is no guarantee that the *right* people will buy into it. In the case of the man in Texas, it looks like he's definitely failed to convince either the authorities or the store itself, which means that all his efforts may have been wasted. If he can just get some jurors to believe him, then it'll have been worth it.

Petey Grew Up

He had been so cute when Mona had first spotted him. She had no idea a baby alligator could be so adorable. On an impulse she decided to buy him. She did that a lot, buying things without thinking about the possible consequences. It never occurred to her that baby alligators grew up to become adult alligators. Her boyfriend, Roger, was appalled when he saw it.

"What is that?" he said, frowning.

"That's Petey. Isn't he cute?"

"No, he's a crocodile. Crocodiles aren't cute."

"He isn't a crocodile, he's an alligator."

"What's the difference?"

"I don't know, but the lady I bought him from said he was an alligator."

"Whatever it is, you've got to get rid of it."

"Why?"

"Do you have any idea how big those things can get? They're dangerous."

"Petey won't be dangerous. He's sweet."

No matter how hard Roger argued with her, Mona just wouldn't accept that someday Petey was going to grow up and became a dangerous creature. So, for her own safety and his peace of mind, he waited for her to fall asleep that night and took the still-tiny Petey and flushed him down the toilet.

That next morning she cried and screamed at him for over two hours before she finally came to her senses and agreed that maybe buying a baby alligator wasn't the most sensible move she had ever made. It didn't take them long to forget about the incident, and they never talked about it again.

Later that year they got married. Mona continued to work at a department store, and Roger got a new job with the department of sanitation. A decade passed and they had two children, a son and a daughter. Roger earned several promotions and was soon the foreman of a crew that looked after 40 square blocks of the public sewer system. Over those 10 years he had come across some very strange items that people had disposed of down there, but he never recalled the bizarre item he had once been responsible for.

For years he had heard the rumors about man-eating reptiles attacking other city workers, but he had been around long enough that he knew they weren't true. His daughter, Fiona, who was eight at the time, once asked him about them.

"Elijah Daniels told me that there are a whole bunch of alligators in the sewers where you work. Is that true?"

Roger laughed, smiled and picked up his daughter and placed her on his lap.

"Honey, do you know what urban legends are?"

She shook her head.

"Well, they're kind of like fairy tales. Only instead of being about fairies, dragons and unicorns, they're about real life. People like to tell them because they're sometimes funny and scary, but only really silly people believe them. Do you understand?"

"I think so."

"The story about alligators living in the sewer system is an urban legend, and you can tell Elijah Daniels that if he really believes it then he's just a silly little boy. I spend a lot of time down there and I've never seen a single alligator. Okay?"

"Okay," she said before she got down from his lap and ran off to play.

Two months later, Roger and Mona were awakened by the sound of their telephone. It was three o'clock in the morning. Groggy and annoyed, Roger picked up the phone.

"It's 3 AM," he groaned into the receiver.

"We got a problem down here," answered the voice on the other end. Roger recognized it as Mason, another foreman.

"What is it?" Roger sat up, knowing that if Mason was calling him at this hour then it must be important.

Mason paused before he spoke.

"Just get over here. You won't believe me until you see it yourself." He told Roger where they were and then hung up.

Slowly, Roger got out of bed and got dressed.

"Where are you going?" Mona muttered into her pillow, still half asleep.

"Mason Bingham needs my help."

"Oh, okay."

As Roger drove down to the location that Mason had given him, he tried to imagine what could happen down in the sewers that was so out of the ordinary that he had to see it before he could believe. He arrived at the address Mason had given him and immediately spotted the yellow gate they used to warn people about an open manhole. He climbed down the ladder into the sewer and heard only silence. He called out to Mason.

"Where are you guys?" he shouted. All he heard was the echo of his voice.

Cautiously he began to move forward. For the first time in 10 years he felt uneasy being in the sewer. There was something unsettling about this situation. He called out to Mason several more times, but he never got an answer.

After 20 minutes he decided to turn back and call his boss, as it was obvious that something was seriously wrong. He turned around and started back. His footsteps echoed ahead of him. From behind him he heard the sound of a loud splashing.

"Mason?" he asked as he quickly turned around, expecting to see his coworker.

He screamed when he saw what was there instead.

All alligators look the same, so he had no way of knowing that the one in front of him was the same one he flushed all those years ago, but it was. Elijah Daniels had been wrong. A whole bunch of alligators didn't live in the sewer system, there was just one, but he was a *big* one. Petey had grown up and up and out and out, easily becoming 10 times the size of a normal alligator. Roger could see blood in the animal's teeth and he knew where it had come from. He turned around and began to run as fast as he possibly could, but it wasn't fast enough. Petey came after him and, turning his head, chomped down on Roger's left leg. The force of his bite was so powerful it severed the leg right off Roger's body.

Screaming, he fell to the sewer's floor and tried to crawl as fast as he could while Petey finished eating his leg. Unfortunately for him Petey was a fast eater and 30 seconds later he went after the rest of his meal.

Over the years that followed, the mystery of the disappearances of Roger, Mason and his crew was never solved. The only clue they had was Mona's insistence that her husband had gotten a late night call from Mason, but some dismissed this as a fantasy concocted by a woman who didn't want to admit that her man had run away from her.

The investigators, who refused to even consider the possibility of a solution that was so obviously inspired by an urban legend, always dismissed rumors that the men had been consumed by a "whole bunch of alligators."

* * *

The idea that alligators can be found living in sewers may very well be the first urban legend I ever heard. I'm happy to say that even in elementary school I refused to buy it. It seemed so silly.

But then silliness has never been enough to get people to instantly dismiss a story as good as this one. Many people remember it because of the 1980 Lewis Teague film *Alligator*, in which Robert Forster played a detective investigating a rash of strange deaths, only to discover they were being caused by the 50-foot long title creature.

The problem with the legend is that it defies the rules of nature. Alligators simply couldn't survive in a sewer environment. Not only would they not be able to handle the low temperatures of northern cities (New York's sewers being the ones most often said to be infested), but they also wouldn't be able to live in an environment infested by the kind of viruses and bacteria commonly found in sewage.

As told, the alligators in this legend wouldn't mutate and become gigantic; they would instead fall ill and die.

3

They're Celebrities, They Deserve It

*I*f, like me, you are a big fan of the glamorous world of show business, then you have become familiar with the phrase "the curse of celebrity." Most often used when describing the events that lead to a famous person's downfall in the public eye, it is a term that causes many people to roll their eyes and mutter, "oh, puh-lease! I wish I were so cursed!"

Most of us dream only of the good things that come from being famous—namely money, respect and recognition—but we seldom ponder the reality that fame can be fleeting and after your spotlight fades you can be left bankrupt and end up a sad living joke.

The curse of celebrity can also take another form. Having a famous name can sometimes mean that you are going to see it in places you never imagined, like an urban legend. The eight stories in this chapter do little to honor the memories of those they describe.

How would Marilyn Monroe feel if she knew people today described her as being almost four times her actual size? What would John Wayne think about people's speculation about the contents of his intestines? And how badly would King Kong take it if he found out that people believed he really could get his butt kicked by a Japanese dinosaur? These are questions we can never answer, but at least we can talk about the legends that allow us to ask them.

That Would Explain the Way He Walked

Among the many reasons people are so quick to believe the stories that make up this book is that they have a vested interest in believing them. Many advocate groups are not above treating an urban legend as a factual story if they think it will help further their cause. This is why, for example, anti-drug proponents in the 1980s often told the story in speeches and presentations of the drugged-out babysitter as if it had really happened (see the story in Chapter Five: Multiple Maniacs). More interested in the moral of the story, these groups are very often willing to ignore a story's lack of credibility if the telling of it helps them attract more supporters.

For years now the more zealous members of the vegetarian community have been quick to warn the world's carnivores of the danger of eating meat by telling an urban legend so outrageous that people believe it just because it sounds so impossible that it must be true. In the beginning the man described in the story was just an anonymous beef lover, but—just as we will see in the case of the legend of the visit from an old friend—it was only a matter of time before it became attached to a famous name.

Given his status as the most manly man to ever be shown on the silver screen, it is only natural that John Wayne would be the star most often named by the tellers of this tale (with Elvis Presley coming in a distant second). Famed for his roles in patriotic war movies and classic westerns, Wayne personified the machismo of the American male of the 1940s and '50s. He was a tall, strong, quiet man who didn't like violence but was more than willing to use it if he had to. His on-screen presence was so mythic he seemed more like someone out of American folklore, like Paul Bunyan or John Henry. He looked and acted like a man who could cut down a whole forest with one swing of an ax and eat a hundred head of cattle in one sitting.

But, according to the urban legend, a man that powerful and capable of such an appetite is still human and can still be undone by the consumption of animal flesh. Because of his heavy meat diet, insists the legend, after Wayne died, the doctors who performed his autopsy were shocked to discover over 40 pounds of undigested meat impacted in his colon (some versions claim the amount was as high as 80 pounds).

Now we all know people who like their steaks. We've seen them chow them down night after night, happily ignoring the vegetables on their plate, but 40 pounds? That sounds impossible! Guess what? It is. The truth is that if Wayne—or anyone else for that matter—tried to move around with just a pound of undigested meat in their colon, they would find the pain so agonizing they would hardly be able to walk more than a few steps. This simple biological fact, though, is not enough to squelch the legend. Just a few months before I started this book I saw it brought up by a vegetarian during a panel discussion on Canadian television. He didn't mention Wayne, and said that it was 30 pounds instead of 40, but he still stated it as if it were a fact.

Beyond science, the legend is also disproved by the facts of Wayne's death. Because he died of cancer at the age of 72, and the cause of his death was never in question, an autopsy was never performed on his body. Plus all you have to do is look at pictures of him that were taken before he passed away. This was not a man with 40 extra pounds in his mid-section, but a gaunt shadow of the colossus he once was.

What the people who spread this legend around might not know is that there is another, more disturbing story regarding his death. In 1956, Wayne appeared in what many film scholars regard as his worst film, a historical epic produced by Howard Hughes named *The Conqueror*. In it Wayne was hysterically miscast as the infamous Mongolian ruler Genghis Khan, and the film that resulted was so hilariously awful that it would be forgotten today if not for a horrible decision made by the filmmakers.

The producers and director were looking for an interesting desert landscape in the United States in which they could film their movie, and they found it in a stretch of land in Utah known as the Yucca Flats. The fact that the land was being used by the military to test nuclear weapons did not deter them in the slightest, as the government downplayed the danger of radiation in the area. It would take decades for the enormity of this mistake to become apparent, but as the years passed, over 150 of the 220 men and women who worked on the film succumbed to the effects of cancer. Included in this total were Wayne and Dick Powell, the film's director, as well as costars Susan Hayward, Agnes Moorehead and William Conrad. And while there are many famous "curses" in Hollywood—included those linked to the *Poltergeist* films and the role of Superman—this, sadly, is the only one that isn't an urban legend.

And the Winner Isn't...

One reason so many people love to watch the Oscars every year is the chance they give us to root for the underdog, whether it's an independent movie that caught everyone by surprise or a writer or performer who came out of nowhere and was nominated for their profession's highest honor. In 2003, the young actor Adrien Brody stunned everybody when he beat Jack Nicholson, Nicolas Cage, Michael Caine and Daniel Day-Lewis for the much-coveted Best Actor Oscar. Despite the fact that it was his first nomination and his four fellow nominees were all former winners (*multiple* winners in the case of Nicholson and Caine), it was his name that was read aloud, and the moment that resulted was one that few people who saw it would forget.

There have been, however, occasions where people have been so shocked by the name that has been read aloud that they cannot help musing that a mistake must have been made and the wrong person received the award. While this backlash is most often the result of petty jealousy or some kind of snobbery, in at least one case it has haunted one Academy Award winner to the point that to this day people insist she didn't really win the Oscar.

In 1992, 20th Century Fox films released an unassuming comedy called *My Cousin Vinny*, directed by Jonathan Lynn and written by Dale Launer. A vehicle designed to showcase the talents of Oscar winner Joe Pesci, the film details the adventures of a middle-aged law-school graduate named Vincent Gambini, who leaves New York to defend his cousin against a murder charge in a small southern town. While the film was well-aided by a surprisingly funny script and an adept lead performance from Pesci, what made it seem different and special was the performance of Marisa Tomei as Vinny's long-suffering girlfriend, Mona, who has agreed to postpone their marriage until the day he wins his first case. Both critics and audiences singled out the actress, who—despite years spent on television and in small film roles—had seemed to come out of nowhere. It didn't take long for a buzz to take hold about her performance, and soon people were suggesting that it might even be good enough to merit an Academy Award nomination, so when the nominations were announced, people weren't surprised to see that she had been included.

Few, however, thought she had a hope of winning. Not only was she the youngest nominee for Best Supporting Actress that year, but she was also the lone American. Seeing this young ingénue pitted against the likes of Joan Plowright (for *Enchanted April*), Miranda Richardson (for *Damage*), Vanessa Redgrave (for *Howard's End*) and Judy Davis (for *Husbands and Wives*), most people figured that she should just be happy that she got nominated at all.

There is an Oscar tradition of having the winners of the previous year's acting awards read out the names of the nominees in their opposite gender category, so that year the Best Supporting Actress award was handed out by the famed character actor Jack Palance—who shocked the world when, after receiving his award for his role as Curly in *City Slickers*, he proceeded to do some one-armed push-ups to prove that Hollywood's seniors were stronger than they may appear. As is the custom, he read out the nominees' names and opened the envelope and announced—to everyone's surprise—that the winner was Marisa Tomei. Stunned, the young actress stood up and walked onstage where she accepted her award and gave a short speech.

Almost immediately the gossip began to flow across Hollywood. It seemed so incongruous that the young upstart could beat the four respected veterans that rumors of a mistake being made began to spread. The most common theory was that the elderly Palance—who, admittedly, did look slightly dazed that night—had become confused and instead of reading the name in the envelope—which is usually said to have been Vanessa Redgrave's—said the first name in the nominee lineup, Marisa Tomei. And despite Academy rules that dictate that a mistake like that is to be corrected immediately on stage by one of the two people backstage who know who the winners are—without any regard to the feelings of the person whose name has been mistakenly been announced—many people believed the rumor.

This rumor soon grew and became the stuff of urban legend, and it eventually had a negative impact on Marisa Tomei's career. After she was in a couple of movies that tried to elevate her to leading lady status but flopped, people started to dismiss her Oscar-winning performance as an over-praised fluke. It would take her nine years to finally prove that her initial acclaim was really deserved, when she was nominated once again for Best Supporting Actress for her performance in the revenge drama *In the Bedroom*. Even though she lost that year to Jennifer Connelly, who won for *A Beautiful Mind*, the fact that her work had been recognized twice by the Academy came close to finally putting the urban legend to rest.

There are still people who insist that a mistake was made that year, but there is a good chance that this has less to do with the actress than the movie she won for. The Oscars are famous for preferring performances in dramatic roles, to the detriment of actors who work in comedy. Even though most performers will insist that working in a comedy is just as hard—if not harder—than working in a drama, there is a perception that for a performance to be worthy of an award it has to be in a meaningful film, something *My Cousin Vinny* definitely isn't. Marisa Tomei won for being funny in a funny movie, and for some that isn't worthy of the recognition she achieved, making this— perhaps—the snootiest of all urban legends.

A Visit from an Old Friend

Just as nature abhors a vacuum, history abhors an anonymous quote. For this reason nearly every witticism that was said in Victorian England, the Roaring Twenties or the 1940s is attributed to Oscar Wilde, Dorothy Parker and Groucho Marx, respectively. It somehow makes the quotes more interesting if they come from someone who was famous rather than some anonymous wag whose name has been lost to time. This same phenomenon often occurs in the world of urban legends where stories that have been around for years are retold to include famous personalities. In many cases these revamped legends become a part of that celebrity's lore and it is left to their biographers to uncover the truth.

The legend of the visit from the old friend has been told many times with a whole cast of different characters, but by far the most well-known version involves two of Hollywood's most infamous golden age bad boys. While he is most famous today for being Drew Barrymore's grandfather, for the first 30 years of the 20th century John Barrymore was considered by many to be the greatest actor alive. Errol Flynn, on the other hand, was never considered that great of an actor, but thanks to his performances in such classics as *Captain Blood* and *The Adventures of Robin Hood*, he was the pre-eminent matinee idol of his time. While they varied widely in terms of talent and box-office appeal, these two actors had one thing in common: alcohol. Both men competed with W.C. Fields for the title of most famous drunk of the era. Thanks to this, and their reputation for wild abandon, it isn't hard to understand why their names are the ones most closely associated with this particular legend.

It was no secret that Errol Flynn idolized Barrymore. From the time he was born in 1909 in Hobart, Tasmania, "The Great Profile"—as Barrymore was nicknamed—was already considered the greatest Shakespearean actor of his time. Flynn dreamed of being as great an actor as his idol, but his stardom came about because of his dashing good looks and he knew it. There was, however, one way in which he could be his idol's equal and that was by living a life as self-destructive as Barrymore's. Thanks to his fame he was able to get to know Barrymore, and the two men become drinking buddies, despite their 27-year age difference.

But their friendship came to an end when, in 1942, a combination of pneumonia and cirrhosis of the liver ended Barrymore's life at the age of 60. Flynn was devastated to see his friend go and went on the bender of all benders. He lamented his idol's passing in more than one of Hollywood's nightclubs, and it was at one of these after-hours bars that two of Flynn's friends came up with a prank that was so unbelievably cruel that Barrymore himself would have reveled in it. They left their drunken friend to wallow in his misery and hightailed it to the mortuary where Barrymore's body was being held. They broke into the building and borrowed the famous corpse and drove it to Flynn's home, where they sat it on a chair facing his front door.

Several hours later, they heard Flynn struggle to open his door. He was so drunk he could barely manage to stand up. When he finally opened his door he was surprised to see someone sitting in his house. Unable to make out who it was, he walked over to the figure and bent over to check him out. It took him a second, but when he recognized that it was the dead body of his old friend he turned away and ran screaming from his house.

* * *

Even though this story is an urban legend, the fact is that compared to some of the other stories (many of which are true) that are told about these two men, it is a relatively tame anecdote. Despite the effect alcohol had on ending his idol's life, Flynn never put an end to his wicked, wicked ways, and he too died as a result, succumbing to a heart attack in 1959. But unlike his old drinking buddy, there is no account of his being abducted from a mortuary to scare a good friend.

An Undeserved Credit

It isn't a cynical indictment of our society to suggest that most people lie on their résumés. Considering the level of competition people face in the job market, it seems almost silly not to tell a fib or two. This is especially true in the world of entertainment where lying on a résumé is so common it's not considered the slightest bit shameful. Actors regularly claim to possess skills such as horse riding and fencing even if they've never seen a real horse up close or ever clasped the handle of a foil. The idea is if they eventually get a part that requires those skills, they can always take a crash course before they have to start filming. The same is true when it comes to listing your previous credits. Most actors are loathe to admit that their only previous experience is playing the third witch in their junior college's production of *Macbeth*, so they invent a credit or two to make it seem like they aren't complete amateurs.

This ploy is so well-known that most casting directors see through it right away, but in one case a young actor's invention was so well chosen that when he shot to fame in the early 1990s, books and websites were all revised to include him in the credits of a film he never appeared in.

It was as a director that Quentin Tarantino became famous, but before he gained cult stardom as the man behind *Reservoir Dogs* and mainstream stardom for his blockbuster *Pulp Fiction*, he was a struggling actor making $4 an hour as a video clerk. Tarantino loved movies, but he had never so much as acted in a school play (he had dropped out in the ninth grade) before he tried to find work as an actor, so he had nothing to put down on his résumé for experience. What he did have, though, was an encyclopedic knowledge of cinema and a job at a video store that carried some of the most obscure films ever made, so he was able to come up with the perfect film to put down as his first job as an actor.

According to Cannes Film Festival legend, the genesis of the movie Tarantino put down on his resume came about during the annual event when the infamous Israeli action movie producer and director Menahem Golan sat down at a table with the even more infamous French film director Jean-Luc Godard. It was an odd pairing to say the least, but the two men hit it off and struck a deal to work together then and there. Godard agreed to film his take on Shakespeare's *King Lear* on the condition that Golan get Woody Allen to play the part of the jester. The two men shook hands, and several months later Allen spent two days filming the part that was so important to Godard. But as easily as the film had come together, the result proved unworthy of the effort. Godard's *King Lear* turned out to be his most incoherent film, and despite the presence of other notable actors such as Molly Ringwald, Burgess Meredith and the writer Norman Mailer, the movie went virtually unreleased in North America (even Allen admitted in interviews that he had never seen it).

Knowing as much as he did about filmmaking, Tarantino sensed that *King Lear* was the perfect film to put down on his résumé. On the one hand, it had been directed by a world-famous master whose movies were much respected by the cinematic community, while on the other hand, it had been seen by so few people that it was almost impossible to prove that he wasn't in it. With his résumé in hand Tarantino was able to find work, securing the role of an Elvis impersonator in an episode of the geriatric sitcom *The Golden Girls.*

But as exciting as that role had been, it wasn't enough to satisfy his hunger for success, so he changed his focus from acting to writing and directing. After some frustrating set-backs he was eventually able to secure financing for his first film, *Reservoir Dogs.* This first effort ended up becoming an instant critical hit, and people started paying attention to the young manic director. This attention proved to be deserved when his second film, *Pulp Fiction,* took the Palm D'Or at the Cannes film festival and became a huge international blockbuster. Interest in Tarantino grew and grew and people started to get their hands on copies of his old resume, which included a credit for his performance in *King Lear.* As various film books and websites were revised, he was included, along with Ringwald, Allen and Meredith, as one of the stars of the film. Fans of Tarantino scoured video stores looking for elusive copies of the film, and those who had actually found it suggested that his role was quite small, nothing more than an eye-blink cameo, but they stopped short of denying he was in it.

Finally Tarantino himself put the legend to rest by admitting that he had lied on his résumé. Those same books and websites that had been so quick to include him took his name out of the movie's credits when they were revised once again. As a result, this is one of the few urban legends about a famous person that was successfully put to rest, but it isn't that hard to find copies of the books that show that many people were easily deceived by the innocent trickery of a struggling young actor.

Choking on the Truth

Almost an hour into the first installment of Mike Myers' popular *Austin Powers* film franchise, the anachronistic English spy/photographer decides to take an inventory of what has happened to his friends since he was put into cryogenic hibernation 30 years earlier. On a list entitled "People I Know" he writes the names of these famous celebrities and is despondent to learn how many of them have died. As he goes down the list he crosses out the names of the deceased and writes down the method of their early demise. Beside Jimi Hendrix's name he writes down "drugs." For Janis Joplin he writes down "alcohol," and when he gets to Mama Cass he doesn't even pause before writing the words "ham sandwich." It's a funny, if slightly morbid, joke, but the truth is that despite the legend that has existed ever since Cass Elliot died in 1974, the death of the famed singer was no laughing matter.

To this day the woman known as Mama Cass Elliot (whose real name was Ellen Cohen) remains one of the unique figures in the history of rock and roll. Blessed with a clear and powerful voice, she sang her way to stardom along with Denny Doherty and John and Michelle Phillips, who— as The Mamas and The Papas—scored with some of the 1960s' most memorable hits, such as "Monday, Monday" and "California Dreamin'." But what set her apart was not her success or her talent, but her size. Standing only 5'5", she weighed (at her heaviest) nearly 300 pounds. This, in a business where her waif-like counterpart Michelle Phillips was considered the norm, was enough to make her one of the most visible figures of her era. Unfortunately, it also made her the butt of many cruel jokes, both during her life and after her death.

Despite this negative attention she was a woman who loved life and wanted to enjoy everything that it had to offer. Her sense of humor was legendary, as was her love of tomfoolery. Her most famous practical joke came at the expense of the Internal Revenue Service, when it declared that she owed them $10,000 in back taxes. Not wanting to face the penalties that could arise from non-payment, she decided to pay what she owed, but not in the way that the I.R.S. wanted. Spending an additional $3000, she rented a truck and filled it with one million pennies ($10,000 worth) and dumped the change beside a dumpster next to the I.R.S.'s building. In the end the joke was on her, because a federal law made it illegal for a person to use more than a quarter's worth of pennies as part of their payment, which put her $9999.75 over the limit. She was cited for contempt and forced to clean up all the loose change.

Sadly, she isn't remembered today for stories like this or even for her music. Instead she is remembered because in 1974, at the age of 32, she died with a sandwich on her bedside table. Exhausted after weeks of touring and enduring an unhealthily strict diet, she had gone to stay at the London home of her friend, songwriter Harry Nilsson, and it was there that she was found two nights after her last performance. When the British papers caught wind of her death, they asked a local physician for a quote regarding how she might have died. Noting the sandwich found on the scene, the doctor suggested that she might have choked to death, and it was from that suggestion that the urban legend began to grow. Even though the doctor who had made the statement had not examined the body and was not even present at the site of her death, his knee-jerk appraisal made it across the ocean, and headlines throughout the U.S. read "Mama Cass Chokes to Death on Ham Sandwich."

If it had been the other female member of The Mamas and The Papas who had been found like this, people would have instantly doubted this version of events. It would be difficult to imagine that a svelte blonde like Michelle Phillips could die while eating, but because the story was about Cass Elliot no one questioned it for a second. It was easy to accept that the famous fat woman had died because of her appetite, and that is why to this day people believe that she really did choke to death.

The truth is that Cass Elliot did die because of her appetite, but not because of a single sandwich. The official cause of her death, as verified by the medical examiners who performed the autopsy on her body, was heart failure. After years of overeating followed by crash dieting, Cass Elliot's heart finally had had enough and gave up. It is hard to imagine that people would find something funny in this real explanation, which is why—for the sake of a good joke—it will never be able to supplant the legend as the popular reason for her death.

In an eerie footnote to this story, Cass Elliot was not the first rock and roll legend to die in the home of Harry Nilsson, who is most famous today for his contributions to the soundtracks for the movies *Midnight Cowboy* and *Popeye* and for his hit song "One (Is the Loneliest Number)." That same year his home also served as the final stop for Keith Moon, the infamous drummer for The Who, who died from an overdose of prescription drugs, which—as Austin Powers' list suggests—is the real way a rock star should go.

A Size Sixteen

Just a few years ago the famous British model and actress Elizabeth Hurley caused a plethora of headlines and op-ed articles to appear when she was quoted as saying that she would kill herself if she were as fat as the great movie icon Marilyn Monroe. Her honest statement of fact was carted out as an example of how unhealthy western culture's idea of beauty had become. What did it say about us if someone as gorgeous as Marilyn couldn't find work today? The most shocking aspect of these articles for many people was the assertion that Marilyn wore a size 16. In an age when many famous stars range between sizes 0 and 4, this was an extremely shocking figure. There is just one problem with it. It isn't true.

Like the legend about what was found inside John Wayne after he died, the enduring myth of Marilyn Monroe's dress size has refused to go away because it allows people to further their specific cause. During a time when many young woman fight against eating disorders, the idea that one of the most celebrated female figures of the 20th century wore a dress that was nearly four times bigger than what Hollywood would now consider too heavy inspires hope that we can someday return to celebrating a more realistic body type. What the legend fails to take into account is that dress sizes have changed drastically over the years, and a size 16 in the 1950s and '60s would be a size 12 today.

But a size 12 is still quite large by Hollywood standards. The trouble is that there is no evidence that Marilyn ever wore a size 16. Her biographical information states that she was 5'5$\frac{1}{2}$", her weight fluctuated between 120 and 135 pounds and her most commonly accepted measurements ranged between 35-22-35 and 37-24-37. These are definitely the measurements of a woman with curves, but they are no way high enough to require that she wear a size 16.

Because of her status as a film icon, many of the costumes she wore have been saved and can be found in museums. In today's sizes, these costumes range between sizes 4 and 7, and while these would put her into the heavier end of today's Hollywood spectrum, they wouldn't make her unemployable.

The easiest way to disprove this legend is simply by watching her movies and looking at her many photographs. She was the first woman to be featured in the centerfold of *Playboy*, and in that famous picture you see a woman who could easily be found today in the very same magazine. Still, it is unlikely that the perception that Marilyn was so much heavier than her present-day counterparts will go away anytime soon, as it is one of those urban legends that make people feel good about themselves, which makes it a rare commodity indeed.

The Ultimate Celebrity Catfight

One of the inevitable risks involved in studying urban legends is the likelihood that you will at some point discover that a story you yourself believed to be true and shared with people is in fact completely bogus. This happened to me several times during the course of my research for this book and I feel honor bound to include one of these legends as it proves that even the most wary and skeptical among us can get caught in the urban legend trap if the bait proves seductive enough.

In the case of this legend, I wasn't even looking for it when I discovered it. I was trying to find stories to go into this chapter about Hollywood, when I found out that a popular bit of movie lore I had shared with many people over the years was—you guessed it—a total urban legend. As a former film student and a fanatical movie buff, I was horrified to learn of my mistake, and even though this urban legend may seem minor compared to others described on these pages I feel I must share it with you in order to hopefully correct the damage I have done. Plus it's a lot of fun to write about really big monkeys.

In 1962 Toho Studios, the legendary Japanese film company, had decided to make a fifth installment in their wildly popular Gojira monster movie series (the monster's name, which was a combination of the Japanese words for gorilla and whale, was changed when the films were released in North America to the more well-known Godzilla). Having had some success in the North American market, the filmmakers decided that it made sense to pit their big lizard against a foe that was a great American hero. They didn't have to think long to decide who this should be, since there was only one American hero big enough to go toe-to-toe with the "King of the Monsters." He too was a king and his name was Kong.

The gigantic ape known as King Kong was the brainchild of 1930s' film producers Merian C. Cooper and Edgar Wallace, two former wrestlers who dreamed of making a film that would be the most fantastic spectacle of all time. Helping them in their quest to meet this goal was Willis O'Brien, a special effects wizard who pioneered the technique known as stop-motion animation. The result was one of the biggest hits of the decade, and though its first weekend gross of $90,000 sounds unforgivably miniscule today, it was enough to set records in 1933. The film became a beloved classic; despite the inevitable sequels and remakes that came later, it has never been duplicated. The appeal of the film comes from the way it makes us sympathize with the plight of the monstrous ape. We care and root for him, even as he kills people in his rampage through New York City. When he falls from the top of the Empire State Building, we do not cheer because the monster has been vanquished, but instead we weep because we know he was just misunderstood.

The filmmakers at Toho knew this only too well and that was why they clearly made King Kong the hero of their film, which was imaginatively entitled *King Kong vs. Godzilla.* But despite Godzilla's obvious role as the film's villain, a legend about the ending of the film became popular among film geeks almost as soon as the film was released. According to the legend, the producers of the film were more than happy to produce a version where Kong proved triumphant, which they sent over to North America, but—not wanting to

wound the pride of the Japanese people—they filmed another version of the movie where Godzilla proved the victor. This version was said to be available only in Japan, where audiences were believed to never be able to accept their beloved lizard losing to a big hairy ape.

As it is not uncommon for film companies to release different versions of movies for different markets, it was easy for most movie lovers to believe that it had happened in this instance. Many books that mentioned the movie frequently took pains to describe the two different endings, and fans tried for years to get their hands on the Japanese version of the movie, but to no avail. There was a good reason it was impossible to find even a bootleg version of the Godzilla-wins edition of the movie, and that was because it didn't exist. The legend was just that, a legend. The ending that was seen in America was almost identical to the one seen in Japan, save for one key difference.

In both versions, the battle ends with the two monsters battling in the ocean as the Japanese army watches. At the climax of the fight the two behemoths dive below the water, and in the end only Kong arises. The last shot of the movie is of Kong swimming away from Japan. Although this may seem like a clear victory for the American, the filmmakers intended it to be a draw. Since Godzilla arose from the ocean's depths in the first place, his staying under the water wasn't a clear indication of his defeat. While this isn't as clear in the American version, it is made obvious in the Japanese, where, as Kong swims away, the distinctive cry of Godzilla is heard over the soundtrack. The truth is that in both the Japanese and American versions, neither monster really won the battle.

Having for years believed that there were two versions of the movie out there, I was disappointed to find out the truth. Not just because it meant I was wrong all those years, but also because, in this case, the truth turned out to be so lame. A draw? That's just weak.

Lose Weight While You Eat

Before the term was taken over by the likes of Jennifer Lopez, Whitney Houston and Mariah Carey, a woman who was a diva was not someone who deigned to sing popular music, she was a woman who sang opera and her voice was so powerful it demanded respect. Among this select group of vocal powerhouses, none was more controversial than Maria Callas. Born in New York City in 1923, but raised for much of her childhood in Greece, she had a voice unlike any other. To this day music critics argue over her status in the world of classical music, some calling her its greatest vocal artist, others suggesting she was vastly overrated and more famous for her public behavior than the quality of her arias. But chances are if you were to mention her name to the type of person who grimaces when they hear the word opera, they will stare at you blankly, unless they know their urban legends. Then they might answer by asking, "isn't she the one who swallowed the tapeworm?"

While the legend of the woman who deliberately ingests the egg of a tapeworm so she can lose weight has been attached to the names of other famous women (most often supermodels and unusually skinny actresses) it is most often associated with Callas. This act of stupendous vanity has become so much a part of her mythos that it is frequently mentioned in newspaper and magazine articles about her and has even popped up in biographies about her by authors who were unwilling to sacrifice a scandalous story for the sake of the truth.

The reason the legend is most often associated with her is that she is one of the only famous stars of the 20th century to have actually hosted one of the parasitic worms. Unlike the other famous women who have been mentioned in the legend, Maria Callas actually suffered from a tapeworm, but not because she wanted to lose weight. Her unfortunate condition was instead one of the risks inherent in the consumption of her favorite dish, steak tartar. This infamous gourmet entree is nothing more than raw ground steak, and one of the dangers of eating raw meat is that it may contain the eggs of these horrible parasites.

The truth is that becoming host to a tapeworm can be so horrific that no sane person would deliberately allow one to live in them, no matter what kind of short-term benefits it might have for the figure. But, then again, in an age when people are willing to undergo invasive and untested plastic surgeries in order to achieve their ideal physical state and when people are willing to inject strains of botulism into their faces to stop wrinkles, it isn't hard to understand why people are so willing to accept this legend at face value. As sad as it sounds it isn't hard to believe that somewhere out there someone has heard this legend and thought to him or herself "I wonder if that would really work?"

4
A Strange Way to Go

I t isn't hard to figure out why there are so many urban legends about death. Along with being born, breathing and a few other mundane actions necessary for human existence, it is one of the few truly universal experiences. We are all going to die. The only variables are how and when. For many of us the best we can hope for is to go quietly and painlessly in our sleep when we're very old, but very often that just doesn't happen. People die every day in bizarre accidents that make us ponder the fragility of our own mortality and make us willing to believe legends about similar kinds of accidents even if the events these stories describe defy logic or are simply impossible.

One of the benefits of these legends is that the incidents they describe are so out of the ordinary that they allow us to relax and feel a little bit safer. The deaths accounted here are so improbable that after hearing about them we can smile and take comfort in knowing that the chances of something like that happening twice are so minute that we have no cause to fear them. That the stories are often so improbable that they have never happened at all doesn't really matter.

Saying Goodbye

Tim literally didn't see it coming. He had been late getting to work that morning, which normally wasn't that big a deal, since he was one of the co-owners of the small accounting firm that he worked at. The problem was that just the day before he had fired a popular but habitually late employee and he was afraid of the whispers his own tardiness might cause as a result. It was because of this that he abandoned his usually sensible driving habits and tore down the freeway at over 30 miles past the limit. Still, as fast as he was going, the accident wasn't his fault.

The driver of the semi that swerved into him had just woken up from a long night of drinking, and his two hours of sleep had not been enough to sober him up. His vision blurred and his reaction time seriously impaired, the trucker almost crashed into four other cars before he slammed into Tim's speeding German import. The sound that resulted was a nauseating cacophony of crashing steel. It happened so fast it was over before Tim was aware it had begun. The truck driver was killed, but Tim was still somehow conscious. He didn't think he was hurt, because he felt no pain, but he was wedged so tightly inside his car that he could barely move.

Within minutes the authorities were on the scene. First the police and then the fire department took turns inspecting the damage as they tried to figure out how to extricate Tim from his crushed vehicle. Horns honked impatiently as frustrated commuters were forced to a standstill behind the accident scene. A middle-aged man got out of one of the cars and walked over to a policeman.

"Excuse me," the man said, "but I was just wondering if you guys could use some medical help? I'm a doctor."

The paramedics had yet to arrive, so the officer in charge, Sgt. Chalmers, thought it might be a good idea to get a doctor's opinion about Tim's situation. The doctor walked over to the car and introduced himself to Tim, whose mood was closer to chagrined embarrassment than anything else.

"Hi Tim," he said. "I'm Dr. Kellogg. Do you mind if I ask you some questions and take a quick look at you?"

"Sure," agreed Tim, "just as long you don't give me a needle. Horrific car crashes I can handle, but needles give me the heebie-jeebies."

Dr. Kellogg laughed politely at Tim's attempt to ease his own tension while he looked at how Tim was pinned into his car.

"Tim?" he asked when he noticed something. "How much pain are you in?"

"None. Why? Should I be?"

The doctor managed to not show his concern on his face, but instead he just shrugged and said "it's just something I have to ask."

He asked Tim a few more questions before he walked back to the officer in charge. Now he let his face show his true emotions and the sergeant knew immediately that something was wrong.

"What is it doctor?"

Dr. Kellogg sighed heavily before he answered.

"Tim is already dead. He just doesn't know it yet."

"What do you mean?"

"He's not aware of it, but his lower half has essentially been torn off his body. It's only because of how he's positioned in the car that he's still alive. Any attempt to move him will kill him."

"Isn't there—" the sergeant tried.

"—No," the doctor interrupted, "his position is the only thing keeping his internal organs inside his body. You move him and he's dead. It's as simple as that."

Sgt. Chalmers nodded stoically at this.

"What do you suggest we do?"

"Do you know if he's married?"

"I can find out."

"Then I suggest you get someone close to him over here as soon as you possibly can."

Fiona, Tim's wife, was doing some laundry when the phone rang. She answered it and was told by a very serious-sounding man that her husband was in an accident and that a squad car was coming to pick her up.

"Is he okay?" she asked as tears bubbled up out of her eyes.

The man on the other line went silent for a moment.

"He feels no pain" was the best answer he could come up with.

Minutes later Fiona heard a siren just outside her house. Still dressed in her pajamas, she ran out of her house and got into the waiting police car. The young policeman at the wheel drove as fast as he could. The police had blocked off traffic on the opposite freeway, which allowed them to drive past the now mile-long traffic jam behind the accident. As they drove she tried to ask him some questions about what had happened, but he just kept telling her that it would be better if she found out when she got there.

She almost became hysterical when she saw the hunk of twisted metal that used to be Tim's car. As soon as the car stopped she jumped out and ran towards it, but Sgt. Chalmers stopped her.

"Mrs. Zulich," he spoke to her gently, "I have to talk to you before you go to him."

"What's happening?" she cried. "No one will tell me anything! Is Tim okay?"

"He feels no pain."

"What does that mean!" she screamed at him in frustration.

"It means he's alive and conscious."

"Is he badly hurt? Has he been paralyzed?"

Over the course of his career, Sgt. Chalmers had told many people that their loved ones were dead, and it was never easy, but this time it was harder than it ever had been before.

"Mrs. Zulich," he started, "your husband should be dead—"

"—So what are you telling me? That this is a miracle?" she interrupted.

"No," he answered patiently. "What I'm telling you is that he should be dead. What that means is that the only thing keeping him alive is the way he's positioned in the car."

"I don't understand."

"Your husband is conscious and he feels no pain, but any attempt by us to move him will kill him."

"So don't move him!" she sobbed, knowing—as she said it and as hundreds of car horns honked just a few feet behind her—that this wasn't possible.

The sergeant let her cry until her tears stopped falling. Finally she was ready to accept the situation as best she could.

"Does he know?" she asked him.

"No," he answered. "We thought it would be best if he heard it from you."

Fiona bit her lip and nodded.

"Can I go to him now?"

"If you want."

She stood still for a moment and looked down at the asphalt at her feet. She stood there until she was able to drown out the noise of the horns and simply hear her own heartbeat. When that was all that she heard, she lifted her head and walked over to the mangled car.

Tim looked annoyed when she first saw him, but his face brightened immediately when he caught sight of her.

"Honey," he greeted her warmly, "why are you still in your pajamas?"

The best she could manage was a small smile.

"What's the matter?" he asked her.

She answered him with a single movement of her eyes.

"Oh, the accident. Right. Has anybody told you anything about how or when they're getting me out of here? I keep asking, but they won't tell me what's going on."

She nodded.

"They were waiting for me," she explained to him.

"Why? Are you going to get me out of here?"

She shook her head; tears started falling down her face.

"What's wrong?"

She took a deep breath and answered him. He stayed quiet for a moment.

"There's nothing they can do?" he asked her.

"No. Nothing."

He paused again as he let this all sink in.

"Okay," he said finally.

This proved too much for her and she lost it once again. Like the sergeant before him, Tim let her cry until the tears stopped coming.

"It'll be okay," he reassured her.

"How can you say that?"

"Because it's true. Everything will be fine." His voice was so sure and calm, Fiona couldn't argue with it.

"I love you," she said to him.

"I know. I love you too."

"I know."

"Now give me a kiss."

Fiona leaned into the wreck and the two of them kissed for one last time.

"Now there's just one last thing," he said to her when they were done.

"What?"

"Have fun."

She just looked at him, confused.

"I'm going to be up there watching you, and if I see you mourning and grieving for a lot longer than is needed, I'm going to be pissed. Have fun. You have years and years left to live your life. If you really love me, you'll do everything you can to enjoy them."

"Okay, I promise."

Tim was still conscious when the Jaws of Life were used to cut away the wreckage that surrounded him. He joked with the men who helped to cut him out. They tried their best to laugh with him, but the reality of the situation made it hard. When they were finally ready to pull him out they asked him if he wanted another few minutes.

"No," he answered. "It's time."

* * *

Of all the urban legends in this book, this is easily the most melodramatic. It's also one of the most thought-provoking, as it asks us to consider what it would be like to know with certainty that you have only a few hours, or even minutes, to live. This is probably why the story had been told several times on film and television.

The most famous version of the legend appeared in the 2002 M. Night Shyamalan hit *Signs*. A reverend played by Mel Gibson is brought to the scene of a car accident, where his wife has become pinned to a tree. He gets there just in time to speak to her before she dies, and with her final words she tells him something that will later save his family.

A less well-known but much more powerful version of the story aired on December 5, 1997, in an episode of the TV show *Homicide: Life on the Street*. Here viewers watched for a full hour as a businessman, played by *Men in Black*'s Vincent D'Onofrio, was pushed in front of a speeding subway train and became pinned between the train and the platform. With the clock ticking, the detectives searched for his girlfriend and for the man who pushed him. Sadly, when the detectives find his girlfriend she assumes that they want her for some minor violations and she runs away and loses them. But the man who pushed him is caught—it turns out he has done this before—and his victim is allowed to berate him for his crime before the police take him away. Finally, after having gone through all the different psychological stages a person experiences knowing the end is coming, the man accepts his fate as gracefully as he can, albeit still a little annoyed that his girlfriend never showed up.

While not as obvious an urban legend as most of the stories in this book—I, myself, assumed that the episode of *Homicide: Life on the Street* was based on a true story the first time I saw it—this story's status as folklore and not fact is proven by its longevity rather than its lack of credibility. The story has existed in some form or another for close to half a century and is constantly being reinvented over the decades. The earliest versions most often involved factory or construction workers who got caught in the machinery they worked with, before branching out of the workplace to other potentially fatal venues. The one thing about the different versions that has always stayed consistent is its air of melancholy fatalism and its suggestion that calm dignity is the right way to go in the end. In an odd way, this is what makes the sad story seem so much more uplifting than its less-enlightened counterparts.

Totally Baked

Shari could not believe what she had just heard.

"Excuse me?" she asked Brittany, sure that she must have said something else.

"Will you be one of my bridesmaids?" asked Brittany, repeating the same inexplicable question she had said before.

If the stunned silence seemed awkward, Shari didn't notice. Brittany was asking her to join the bridal party for a wedding in which the groom was Shari's ex-boyfriend, Tyler, who had dumped her for Brittany four months before, after they had been engaged for four years. The sheer audacity of Brittany's request was enough for Shari to briefly question her own sanity.

The two of them had grown up together and had been best friends since the third grade. They had gone through adolescence together unscathed, without falling to the pitfalls that can dash young friendships to pieces when puberty raises its pimply head, and had pledged to each other that their bond was eternal when Brittany moved away to go to a school on the east coast. Every attempt was made to keep their friendship alive, but separated as they were by thousands of miles, they eventually lost contact with each other and spent the next decade without hearing from each other. Then one day Brittany called Shari out of the blue and told her that she was back in town and would love to get together with her. Shari's sister, Aurora, was having a birthday party that night, so she invited her long-lost friend to attend.

"I can't wait for you to meet my fiancé, Tyler," she had told her, "I think you'll like him a lot."

It turned out that she was right. Brittany did like Tyler a lot, and Tyler liked Brittany even more. The two of them ended up spending the whole night talking to each other, and when the party died out Shari was astonished to discover that they had left together. Tyler called her and ended their engagement the next day. Two months later she found out that he and Brittany were engaged. Another two months passed before she got the call from Brittany that had led to this meeting at an Italian restaurant, where Shari was still sitting in stunned disbelief and trying to come up with an answer to her great betrayer's question.

"No" was the best she could come up with.

"That's okay," responded Brittany, "you don't have to give me your answer right away."

"I'm not going to do it," Shari insisted.

"I understand that you are still a bit angry with me and Tyler, but it would mean the world to us if you were involved in our wonderful day. After all, without you we may never have met. So just think about it a few days and tell me then."

Shari wasn't sure if Brittany was deliberately being obtuse, or if she had a brain tumor that affected her ability to understand others.

"I don't have to think about it. There is no way I am going to have anything to do with anything that might make you two happy."

"Great! So, I've got to go," Brittany said as she pulled out some cash for her half of the check. "Call me some time next week and let me know, so I can order a dress in your size."

With that she got up and walked out of the restaurant.

The other diners tried their best to ignore Shari as she let out a loud scream of fury and frustration. As soon as it left her mouth, all the energy drained out of her body and she slumped onto the table with her head buried in her folded arms. It was in this position that the devil that lived on her left shoulder began to whisper into her ear.

"Do it! Be one of her bridesmaids!" the devil whispered.

"What? Why would I do that?" she asked it.

"Think about it. What's the best way to get revenge on that lady Judas?"

"I don't know."

"Ruin her wedding! And what's the best way to do that?"

"Make rude noises during the vows?"

"No! Steal Tyler away from her, like she stole him from you!"

"But how?"

The devil told her.

Later that night Shari called Brittany and told her that she would be more than happy to be one of her bridesmaids. Brittany responded to this by shouting with glee.

"I knew I could count on you!" she gushed. "Now I need to know what size dress you wear, so I can order one right away."

Shari gave her a number.

"Really?" asked Brittany. "I would've guessed you were bigger than that."

Shari was, by two sizes, but she insisted the number she gave was correct.

This was a part of the plan that her own inner devil had whispered to her earlier that day. It was a plan so simple and foolproof that even her own inner angel couldn't find a fault in it. Shari was going to steal Tyler back by looking better and hotter than he had ever seen her before. And in order to make this plan a reality Shari was going to have to drop two dress sizes, undergo a major fashion and cosmetic makeover, get a killer tan and buy contacts. She had just 37 days to get the job done, and she wished she had a couple of months more so she could squeeze in some plastic surgery, but no matter what, she was going to be the most alluring and beautiful woman at that wedding. Even if it killed her.

Her plan started that night when she spent two hours working out to an exercise tape that had still been wrapped in plastic, even though she had bought it six years before. After she was finished she allowed herself to dine on only water and three stalks of celery. Her enraged and empty stomach growled at her furiously all through the night as she slept, but her dreams of revenge were loud enough to drown it out.

Shari devoted herself purely to weight loss that first week. Before and after work she would exercise until she collapsed, and then she would get up and exercise some more. She drank water by the gallon and limited her daily caloric intake to the double digits. For a second she became intrigued by the idea of deliberately swallowing a tapeworm egg to help her process when she discovered it had helped a famous opera singer, but she decided that the worm probably would take longer than she had to grow enough to be effective. She became so obsessed that by that Friday the only thing keeping her alert enough to make it through the day was her desire to humiliate her former best friend, but she knew her suffering was worth it, as she was becoming noticeably thinner.

The next week she allowed herself just enough food to keep herself from falling asleep as she walked around. She also cashed in all her stocks and bonds and sold everything she had that was worth anything. With the wad of cash she accumulated she went to the most expensive and exclusive salon in town. She walked out of it a lot poorer but infinitely more glamorous. Her bland brown hair had been transformed into a vibrant red that cascaded down in soft ringlets around her face, which had been reinvented with a host of innovative makeup techniques. She marveled as she looked at herself in the mirror. She looked like one of those old-fashioned movie stars, only in color and thinner.

She had just 13 days to go when she realized she had forgotten to work on her tan, which was a very important part of the package. Brittany sported a beautiful even tan, which was odd considering the 10 years she had spent on the gloomy east coast. It was obviously a result of the old fake and bake, and Shari knew she had to get her own butt to a tanning salon fast if she was going to best it. When she tried to book the number of hours she assumed she needed at one salon, they refused, insisting that it wasn't safe to spend that much time in one of their booths in just two weeks. She settled for one quarter of the time she had requested, and then went to three other places to order the same amount.

During that time she had one of the other bridesmaids deliver her dress. She didn't pick it up herself because she didn't want Brittany or Tyler to see what she looked like before the wedding. The dress was as awful as she had feared. Brittany definitely seemed to believe in the dictum that the bride should be the only woman in the wedding party who doesn't look like an idiot. But the calculating young bride hadn't counted on the fact that Shari was a talented seamstress and within a matter of hours the billowy tangerine monstrosity she had chosen had become a sleek and sexy tangerine showstopper. It turned out that Shari had lost so much weight that she even needed to take it in by another two sizes.

With just six days to go before the wedding, Shari was concerned about how long the tan she dreamt about was taking to become a reality. She upped her regime by adding another two salons to her schedule, meaning that she was going to six places every day.

For the same reason she had someone else pick up her dress, she also didn't go to Brittany's staggette, shower or wedding rehearsal. For each she called in at the last minute and insisted that she was too swamped by work to attend.

Finally the big day came and Shari was astonished by what she had done in just five weeks. She literally looked like a new woman. She was four sizes smaller, her skin was a beautiful dark mocha tan and she made Brittany look like a pale man-stealing cow. In her reinvented bridesmaid dress she looked like a model in a fashion magazine, and she couldn't wait to get to the church.

When she got there the reaction was exactly what she had hoped for. Brittany nearly fainted when she saw her old friend walk up to her.

"Shari," she stuttered, "you look..." she struggled for words.

"What?" Shari feigned innocence. "Do I look different?"

Brittany glared at her, having figured out Shari's ruse, but instead of calling her on it she just sniffed the air and commented on a strange odor that was lingering around them.

"What is that?" she wondered aloud. "It smells like it's coming from you," she told Shari.

Shari couldn't smell anything, so she just assumed that the bested bride was merely being catty.

Heads turned and people whispered as Shari made her way down the aisle. Tyler did a triple take when he saw her walking towards him. She smiled at him seductively before turning and standing in her spot. As the ceremony continued it became clear that her initial hope of seeing Tyler end the wedding right there wasn't going to happen, but she wasn't crushed, since she knew it would be easy to corner him during the reception and convince him he had made a mistake that day. She smiled sweetly as she imagined Brittany alone at the reception hall looking for him, just as Shari had done at her sister's birthday party all those months ago.

Several times during the long ceremony both the reverend and members of the wedding party found themselves sniffing the air, trying to recognize the strange smell in their vicinity. Shari seemed to be the only person who didn't notice it.

The ceremony ended and Shari spent the next few hours biding her time and waiting for just the right opportunity to make her move on Tyler. Finally, after the cake had been cut and the bouquet and garter had been thrown, Shari was able to grab Tyler away from his new bride.

"What are you doing?" he protested as he pushed her away from him when she tried to kiss him.

Shari was completely unprepared for this reaction. She had expected him to become instantly inflamed by the power of her new appearance, but he just looked at her with contempt. Before he turned to leave he noticed the same odor in the air that everyone had smelled during the ceremony.

"Is that coming from you?" he asked her, but before she could deny it he turned and walked away from her.

Alone and rejected, Shari felt cheap and incredibly hungry. It was also at that moment that she finally noticed the smell that Tyler had just commented on and that had been itching the noses of the wedding party all day. He was right, she realized, it was coming from her.

A week passed and the smell would not go away. It was a heavy, meaty smell that most people would never think could possibly emanate from a human body. It smelled like someone was making a soup using all the parts the butcher had to throw away because even the pet food companies wouldn't touch them. She tried to wash it away with multiple bathings, even resorting to using tomato juice a couple of times—like you were supposed to when you got zapped by a skunk—but it would not go away. She tried to mask it by using strong perfumes, but they just intermingled with the smell to create an even more unpleasant aroma. Her coworkers began to avoid her and it became clear to her that she had to go to a doctor to find out what was wrong.

The doctor had never seen—or rather smelled—anything like it before. He ordered up a whole slew of different tests, hoping that one of them might give him a clue about this mysterious ailment. Shari had to wait two days for the results to come in, and during that time the smell became so bad she couldn't leave the house until she had to leave for the doctor's office.

She did not like the look on his face when he came in to talk to her that morning. He stared down at the test results and pulled a chair over to the exam table she was sitting on. He sat down and frowned before he asked her a question.

"Shari, how did you get your tan?" he asked her. "Is it natural or did you go to a tanning salon?"

"A salon," she answered, choosing not to pluralize the noun, like she should have.

"Uh-huh," he nodded. "Did you do it over a long period of time or very quickly?"

"Pretty quickly," she admitted.

"Okay," he looked down at his test results. "Did you also go on a diet during this time?"

"Yes," she answered, as she wondered where this was going.

"I see," he said as he put down his clipboard. "That does explain it."

"Explain what?" she asked anxiously.

The doctor paused as he tried to find the best way to break it to her.

"Shari," he attempted, "I'm afraid that you have done something I have never seen before in my 30 years of practice. I can't find anything like it in any of my textbooks. In fact it is a condition so new and rare that it will probably be named after you."

"What is it?" Shari began to turn pale.

"Thanks to the combination of your poor diet and overexposure to tanning booth radiation, you have...well...the only phrase I can come up that really describes it is that you have cooked your insides."

"What?"

"The best I can sort it out, the tanning booths acted as a sort of microwave, and all that time you spent in them resulted in your internal organs being roasted inside your body. This is what is causing that smell."

Shari stared at him in stunned disbelief.

"Am I going to die?" she finally managed after it all sank in.

"Shari," the doctor replied, deciding not to sugarcoat it, "I'm frankly amazed that you're still alive right now." He shook his head and handed her the test results. "Based on these, the best life expectancy estimate I can give you would have to be measured in hours."

The doctor turned out to be wrong here. Shari lived for a whole week after her diagnosis. Her sister had decided on an open casket for her funeral and everyone who attended, including Brittany and Tyler, agreed that she made for one of the most beautiful and glamorous corpses they had ever seen.

* * *

Like many people, I have two very distinct reactions when I see a person with a dark suntan. The first is that the person looks fit and healthy, which is probably thanks to the hours they spend outdoors pursuing such noble activities as running triathlons and building houses for the homeless. My second—and more strongly felt—reaction is to wonder if the person with the tan has any idea that he or she is just begging for a malignant melanoma.

The irony of a good suntan is that many people get one because it makes them look like they care about their body and live an exciting life, when the truth is that they probably got it by spending 15 minutes in a claustrophobic booth, and they risk serious future health problems by doing so. Throughout history, mankind has fought many battles between our vanity's strange compulsions and our continued survival. Like the women who taunted death by wearing unforgiving tight corsets in the past, today's suntanners are gambling with their lives in the name of fashion. The same ultraviolet rays that cause our skin's melanin count to increase and darken our skin can also cause cancer of the fatal and non-fatal varieties.

So, given that the potential hazards of suntanning are proven medical facts, is Shari's fate in the above story an actual possibility? If you've been paying attention to these stories then you should know by now that the answer to that question is no.

The first accounts of this legend sprung up in the late 1980s when tanning salons grew in number around the continent the way coffee shops did in the '90s. While tanning booths had been around for decades, it was during this period that they became most widely accepted, with many of these salons advertising themselves as a quick and easy way to get a good tan. These businesses took great pains to focus attention on the positive aspects of tanning, but fear of possible litigation also forced them to restrict the amount of time their customers spent in the booths. It is most probably thanks to this that the legend of the woman who died from too much tanning started to grow.

The problem with the legend, as it is told, is that ultraviolet radiation is not capable of cooking a person from the inside. Microwaves, on the other hand, are capable of such a feat, but there has yet to be a single booth ever produced that depended on these waves to give a person a tan. The reason for this is simple: it would not work.

Now if the story ended with Shari going to the doctor a few months, or even years, after her tanning overdose, where she was told that the dark growth on her back proved that she had a possibly fatal case of skin cancer, then the legend would be harder to disprove. Still, as a morality tale warning against the dangers of jealousy and vanity, this legend definitely gets the job done the way it is.

Taking a Big Leap to Get Ahead

Arthur waited nervously as he sat in his boss' office. For the first time since he had started working at the company he was afraid that his job was on the line. Ever since Mr. Gingold had retired and was replaced by Dennis Savage, a narcissistic yuppie who cared only about his next career move, no one in the department felt secure. Mr. Gingold had understood that no one could be perfect and that mistakes were an inevitable part of the process, but Savage only saw the bottom line and how it reflected on him to the higher-ups, so he had no problem firing people for something that was out of their control. Arthur didn't have to worry about that. Since Savage took over, his record had been perfect. But he had another reason to be concerned.

He was old. He was the closest to retirement out of everyone at the office, and Savage, at 34, had nothing but disdain for anyone older than 50 who wasn't an executive. He thought they were dinosaurs who lacked the ambition the company needed to make the stock grow and his own bank account richer.

To his left, Arthur heard the sounds of a toilet flushing and running water come from Savage's personal bathroom. A second passed, and Savage walked out, wiping his hands with a white hand towel.

"Hey, Arthur," he grinned as he walked towards his desk. He dropped the towel onto the floor and noticed Arthur looking down at it. "Don't worry," he said, "that's why I have Enid."

Enid was Savage's secretary.

"So," Savage sighed as he sat down in his expensive leather chair, "what can I do for you?"

Arthur looked confused.

"You wanted to see me," he reminded his boss.

Savage stared at him blankly while he tried to remember if he had called down for the older man or not. He couldn't remember, so he hit the button on his intercom.

"Enid," he spoke into it, "did I ask you to send Arthur over here?"

"Yes, sir," she answered back.

"Why did I do that?"

"I don't know, sir. You didn't say."

"Maybe I've got it written down somewhere," he admitted as he dug through a pile of papers occupying a corner of his expensive mahogany desk. He searched for a second before he found what he was looking for.

"There we go," he said, smiling triumphantly before he looked down at what it said. "Oh, right," he nodded as it all came back to him, "you're fired."

"Excuse me," asked Arthur, afraid that he had misheard.

"You're fired," Savage repeated gracelessly.

"But why?"

Savage scrunched up his face as he tried to remember. He looked down at the piece of paper in front of him.

"It doesn't say," he admitted, "but I'm sure I have a good reason. I'm not the type of guy to do this sort of thing randomly."

"But…but…" Arthur stuttered, "I'm only nine months away from earning my pension!"

"Yeah," Savage nodded, "it's too bad about that, but," he shrugged, "these things can't be helped."

Arthur felt himself starting to shake, and tears started to stream down his face.

"Well," Savage said as he stood up suddenly, "I've got a lunch meeting with the chairman, so I'll let you be alone for a while." He hit the intercom button one more time.

"Yes, sir?" asked Enid.

"I just want to let you know that Arthur is going to need a few minutes of alone time, so could you give him 15 minutes before you call security and make him clear out his desk?"

"Yes, sir."

Before he walked out of his office he patted the inconsolable Arthur on the shoulder.

"Don't worry," he smiled, "you'll bounce back from this somehow."

With that he left Arthur alone to wallow in his despair.

As he wept, a hundred thoughts began to torment his mind. He and his wife, Betty, had counted on that pension for their retirement. They still had a son in college and they had just bought a new car and had been saving for a trip to Europe. Now Nathan would have to drop out, the car was going to be repossessed and their trip money would have to go towards their bills. He knew he was too old to find a job as good as this. The job market was tight enough for kids just out of college, much less for men in their late 50s.

He couldn't do this to Betty, he decided. She didn't deserve to be dragged down with him just because she was unfortunate enough to be his wife. He figured that even if the insurance company refused to pay out his life policy because he committed suicide, she would still be able to find someone else to take care of her. Years of aerobics had allowed her to keep her figure, and she was the best cook in the world. Any successful man his age would be insane not to marry her.

With this in mind he opened the window to Savage's office and walked out onto the ledge. He closed his eyes and leaned forward. The last thing he remembered was the wind whistling past his face.

When he woke up he was in an expensive-looking hospital room. All of his limbs were encased in plaster casts and elevated above his head by a series of pulleys. His body ached and he felt woozy from whatever drugs they had pumped into him, but he was conscious enough to see that Betty was in the room with him.

"Arthur!" she practically screamed when she saw that he was awake.

"Betty," he groaned with pain, "what happened?"

"You fell."

"Fell?"

"Yes, you were in your boss' office and you tripped over his chair and fell out of his open window."

That didn't sound quite right to him.

"Who told you that?" he asked.

"Mr. Hersholt," she told him.

"The chairman?"

"That's right. Actually he's here right now. I'll go get him."

"Uh, okay," Arthur managed to utter before she ran out of the room.

During the time he was alone he took a good long look at his room and decided that there was no way he could ever get one this nice with his medical plan.

A few minutes later Mr. Hersholt, the chairman of the board of Arthur's former employer, walked into his room. He was a tall and dignified man in an expensive suit straight from Saville Row.

"Arthur," he greeted the invalid warmly, "how are you feeling?"

"Fine, I guess," Arthur answered, too confused to complain about the pain.

"Good. Good," the chairman nodded. "So did your lovely wife tell you what happened?"

"She said I tripped."

"That's right."

"But, I didn't—" Arthur tried to explain, before he was interrupted.

"—Memory is a funny thing, Arthur. Now I know that you remember jumping out of Mr. Savage's window because he had terminated your position with the company, but I'm afraid that your recollection just doesn't match up with Ms. Hanson's and my own."

"Ms. Hanson?"

"You would know her better as Enid, Mr. Savage's secretary. She and I walked into his office just as you tripped over his chair."

"But—" Arthur protested.

"Beautiful woman, isn't she?" Mr. Hersholt interrupted him with a strange non sequitur.

"Who?"

"Ms. Hanson, of course."

"Yes, I suppose so."

"I think so to. She's the type of woman a powerful man could fall in love with."

"If you say so."

"I do. I certainly do. However, many powerful men, such as myself, are not free to embrace this kind of love, what with our positions in society and our families. You understand."

"Sure."

"But sometimes powerful men such as myself are not capable of controlling their feelings, and find themselves running towards that very embrace they should avoid."

"Okay."

"And on those occasions they are sometimes caught in this embrace by ambitious young go-getters, who have no compunction using their discovery for their own advancement."

Arthur was beginning to catch on.

"Would Mr. Savage be one of those ambitious young go-getters?" he asked.

"You're very perceptive, Arthur. Very perceptive. Mr. Savage was in fact the mold from which these men were made."

"He said he was going to have lunch with you before he left."

"Yes, we were scheduled to meet."

"Did you have any idea what he wanted to talk to you about?"

"I do believe I had an inkling, but I will never know for sure."

"And why is that?"

"Well, fate is a funny thing, isn't it? Who could imagine that as you tripped and fell out of his office, he would be on the sidewalk below on his way to lunch."

"You don't mean?"

"I do. I most certainly do. You can thank him for saving your life. That is, if he were still alive to enjoy your gratitude. Now, you have a long way to go on your road to recovery, but I hope your journey is made more pleasant by the comforts afforded to you in this private hospital. The company, of course, will see to all your expenses, and we look forward to when you are well enough to come back to work."

"I'm not fired?"

"Of course not. In fact, you've just been promoted. Mr. Savage's untimely passing has left a vacancy at the company. One that I'm certain you'll be more than happy to fill."

"Yes, sir!"

"Good. I'll let you rest now. But before I go, let me ask you just one question."

"Yes, sir?"

"If you knew that Ms. Hanson had taken to embracing someone several years her senior, what would you do?"

Arthur didn't have to think about this one.

"I don't think I'd be capable of knowing something like that, sir," he answered.

"Glad to hear it," Mr. Hersholt clapped his hands together, "now I must be off. I'll send your lovely wife back in."

"Thank you, sir."

"No," the chairman smiled, "thank you."

* * *

One of the unfortunate results of the recent trend towards corporate globalization is that many companies now take a greater interest in the bottom line than the welfare of their employees. In the past many companies did everything they could to avoid letting people go, as their workers were considered a vital part of their corporate family, but today it isn't uncommon for a profitable company to lay off thousands of its employees just to make its shares go up a few more points on the stock market. It is thanks to this new mentality that legends like this one have become so popular in the past decade or so.

What sets this legend apart from others set in the new rat race is its ironic optimism. Arthur's success comes as a direct result of an accident caused by his attempted suicide. Had the callous Savage not fired him, he would have likely spent the rest of his career exactly where he was. So, just as the story serves as an example of the often surreal and maddeningly random machinations of the corporate hierarchy, it also works as a bizarrely uplifting representation of the notion that every cloud has a silver lining.

And while the likely result of Arthur's hurtling body slamming into the surprised Savage would be of two dead men and not just one, this is a hard story to disprove. The irony of its conclusion has the air of obvious fabrication, but stranger things have happened. Still, the lack of any serious reportage on the story places it firmly in the realm of legend, the kind of legend you wish were true.

Aiding and Abetting

There are some stories the detectives tell over and over again. Some are about the hilarious stupidity exhibited by a perp or how a random fluke blew a case wide open. Some are just funny, while others—the ones they save for when last call has been announced—are much more serious. No matter how many times these stories have been told, everyone listens and reacts to them as if they were being told for the first time, laughing at the funny ones and sadly staring into their beers during the others. Out of all the stories they tell, there is only one that makes them do both.

They couldn't help getting somber whenever they talked about a case that involved Garrison. The best detective in their unit, he had been found murdered in the parking lot of the building they worked in every day. The crime was still unsolved, and invoking his name automatically reminded them of their failure to find justice for their fallen friend. But there was one case he solved that was simply too bizarre for them not to laugh and holler at whenever they retold it. It was easily the strangest murder case any of them had ever heard of.

Garrison had been called down to the Fleetwood Arms, a rundown apartment building in the oldest part of town. The body of a 17-year-old boy had been found in the nets that a crew of window washers had set up on one side of the building. As a crime scene, the net was too dangerous to investigate, so by the time Garrison got there the body had already been taken down and sent to the morgue. Jenson, the forensics expert, filled him in on the details.

"The super in this place identified the kid. Said his name was Billy Settler. He lived here with his folks. A couple of uniforms are up there interviewing them right now."

"How do you think he got up there?" asked Garrison.

"The windows in this place don't open," answered Jenson, "which means the only way the kid could have gotten onto the net is from the roof."

"A jumper?"

Jenson shook his head.

"I don't think so."

"He was pushed?"

"Probably not."

"I don't understand."

"Well," said Jenson, "we'll know more after talking to the coroner, but I'm guessing he was forced off the building by the shotgun blast."

"He was shot?"

Jenson nodded.

"In the chest. It would have killed him instantly."

"Did anyone hear it happen?"

Jenson shrugged.

"This isn't a good neighborhood. People hear gunshots all the time. Plus most of the people in this building are seniors. They all have their televisions up so loud it'd be a miracle if they heard someone fire a shot into their own chests."

The building's elevator was broken, which meant Garrison had to walk all the way to the building's second-to-last floor to see the kid's parents. They were an older couple, in their 60s. Billy must have been a late surprise. His father wore blue sweatpants and a white T-shirt, while his mother wore a floral print housecoat that looked to be 20 years old.

They were screaming at each other and at the policemen who were searching the apartment and trying to interview them when Garrison, out of breath from the long trek up the stairs, walked in on them.

"Look, another one!" shouted the woman as he came in. "Why are you bothering us when you should be finding out what happened to Billy?"

Garrison chose not to answer her. Instead he motioned for one of the uniformed officers, a kid just out of the academy, to catch him up on what was going on.

"Why is it so dark in here?" he asked.

The kid shrugged.

"We tried to open the blinds, but I guess they're broken."

"So what've you guys learned?"

"Nothing much, except that these are two of the most miserable people on the planet."

"How'd they react to the news?"

"They screamed at us, but that's not so strange, since that's all they seem to do."

"I found something!" another officer shouted from a bedroom. He came out with a piece of paper and handed it to Garrison.

"What is it?" asked the kid.

"Looks like a suicide note," answered Garrison.

It appeared that young Billy had been a very unhappy boy. His handwritten letter described a lifetime spent with two people who were incapable of anything but furious and nonstop bickering. His parents' constant battles had made him so cynical and doubtful about the possibility of his own future happiness that he decided to end his life rather than risk the possibility of becoming just like them.

Jenson, who was in a lot worse shape than Garrison, finally lumbered into the apartment. He was so tired he had to sit down. He gasped to catch a breath while Garrison walked over to him and handed him the note.

"What do you make of this?" he asked the expert.

Jenson continued to wheeze as he read the note.

"Huh," he responded when he finished reading it. "That's interesting."

"Could he have shot himself on the roof?" asked Garrison.

"Yeah, but there's just one problem with that scenario."

"What?"

"We didn't find a shotgun on the roof, on the net or anywhere along the side of the building."

"So he wrote a suicide note, but somebody else shot him?"

"He could have gotten a friend to do it."

"Look at the note again. He didn't have any friends."

"Right. What about—" Jenson nudged his heads towards the parents.

"That would be my first guess."

"Why is it so dark in here?"

"Blinds are broken."

A couple of hours later Garrison was standing in the morgue with his least-favorite person in the world, Hamilton, the coroner. He had taken Billy's parents in for questioning, but they were so belligerent, he decided to let them sit for a while and calm down. In the meantime he needed to find out what kind of clues Billy's remains could give them.

"He definitely died from the shotgun blast," the balding pathologist informed him. "He was hit directly in the chest, and his heart and lungs were instantly turned into jelly. He must have been quite close to the window when it went off."

Garrison looked at him, confused.

"What do you mean?"

"Judging by the amount of glass I dug out of him, I'd have to say he was just a few inches away."

"But he was shot on top of the roof," Garrison informed him. "There are no windows up there."

Hamilton shook his head and stood by his initial assessment.

"Someone shot this kid through a window."

Garrison drove back to the building. He walked around it and looked for any broken windows. He couldn't find one, but—during his second trip around—he noticed an American flag draped over one of the windows. This wasn't too uncommon, but the fact that the flag was on the outside of the window was. He sighed when he realized what apartment the window came from.

The apartment was quiet now that Billy's parents weren't there anymore. He opened the door and ducked under the yellow crime scene tape to walk inside. He strode over to the heavy blind that had kept the apartment so dark just a few hours before when the sun was out. Pulling as hard as he could he yanked it down and exposed a shattered window, covered by an American flag.

He was walking down the stairs on his way to confront Billy's parents when he was stopped by the voice of teenager. It was a boy, around 13 or 14.

"Mister?" asked the boy. "Are you here about what happened to Billy?"

"That's right," Garrison told him.

"He was shot, right?"

Garrison nodded.

The boy bit his lip and paused before he spoke again.

"I didn't say nothing before, when the policeman came and asked my mom some questions," the boy admitted, "'cause I didn't want to rat on Billy, but then I thought it could help you…"

"Go on."

"Me and Billy were friends. Kinda. He was really quiet most of the time, but we liked the same comic books so sometimes he and I hung out together. We usually just talked about the comics and TV shows we liked, but I remember one day he started talking about his parents."

"What'd he say?"

"He said he hated them. He didn't like how they were always fighting. He said it got so bad that sometimes one of them would grab a shotgun and point it at the other one. He said it didn't mean anything, since it wasn't loaded and there was no ammunition to put in it, but they still acted like they were going to shoot each other. Then he got this weird look on his face, like he had an idea. I think it was the first time I ever saw him smile. He laughed and said that he should buy some ammo and load it into the gun. That way the next time they fought, one of them would end up shooting the other like they wanted."

"Did he do it?"

"I dunno. I didn't talk to him after that."

Billy's father was slumped down on his chair when Garrison burst into the room in which he was being held.

"Where's the gun?" he shouted at the older man.

The old man started to protest, but before he could finish Garrison pounded the table between them with his fist. This stunned Billy's father into silence.

"I know about the shotgun. What did you do with it?"

Once again, Garrison found himself back at the apartment. He walked down into its basement, which served as a storage area for the tenants. He found the cage reserved for the Settlers and opened a trunk that sat on its floor. Under a pile of old clothes and sheets he found what he was looking for.

Jenson was positive.

"This is it," he insisted. "This is the gun that killed Billy, and his mother's prints are all over it."

"Okay. So she shot him while he was outside their window, which has no ledge or any other visible means of support."

"Looks like it."

"And how did she do that?"

Jenson had no idea.

"Magic?" was the best he could come up with.

With this evidence Garrison had enough to book both Mr. and Mrs. Settler, so he decided to let them stew in the lock-up while he went home to get some much-needed sleep. But the puzzle in front of him was too complex to let his mind rest. Instead he just lay there and tried to figure it out. Finally exhaustion overcame him and he fell asleep and started to dream. But then, suddenly, his eyes opened and his body become so energized with excitement he virtually leapt out of his bed.

The answer was so obvious that it seemed impossible.

"You're joking, right?" asked Jenson, when he heard Garrison's theory.

"Think about it."

Jenson frowned.

"I'm still going to go with magic," he decided.

Mrs. Settler looked uncomfortable out of her floral-print robe, which had been exchanged for an orange jumpsuit. She could barely contain her fury when she saw Garrison walk in to talk to her.

"How dare—" she started before he silenced her with a glare.

"I know what happened," he told her. "I know you didn't kill him on purpose. It was just an accident."

She tried to speak, but her emotions caught up with her and she started to sob.

"I didn't know it was loaded," she admitted as tears flooded her eyes.

"You were just threatening your husband like you always did."

"I was so angry at him. He wouldn't shut up. Whenever I got the gun out, he'd usually get the point. I didn't know…we didn't keep any bullets for it! How could I have known?"

"It just went off, didn't it?"

"Right in my hands. There was this blast of noise and the window exploded. I didn't know."

Of all the reports Garrison had written up, this was easily the hardest to sort out. It told the story of a very sad teenager who decided to commit suicide by jumping off his building. He was so angry at his parents for making his life so hard, he decided to leave them with a surprise that might take one of them with him. But no one could have ever imagined that—as he fell towards the ground—his gift would be discovered and blow a hole through his own chest during the split second it took for him to pass by his parents' window on his way down. Garrison noted that, because of the net in which he was found, Billy's suicide attempt would have been a failure. If it were not for the gunshot, he would have survived.

His parents were both changed with manslaughter, and—as the person responsible for loading the gun that killed him—Garrison listed Billy as an accessory in his own murder.

Whenever the detectives finished telling this story, they would all ask each other if they would have had the same epiphany that allowed Garrison to solve the case. Emboldened by a few beers they would all agree that it might have taken them a bit longer, but they would have gotten there in the end. They all knew that this probably wasn't true, but they liked to believe it anyway.

* * *

For most of the 20th century, urban legends usually depended on word of mouth to spread across the globe. While effective, this method is also very slow. It could take years for a story to spread from one coast to another, but that all changed when the Internet grew from being a playground for a select group of computer enthusiasts—a.k.a. geeks—to an important part of normal people's everyday lives. Now, with a single email capturing people's imaginations enough to have them forward it to all their friends, a legend could gain national and international renown in a matter of weeks, if not days.

That habit of sending amusing emails to one's friends and coworkers has resulted in a great number of famous legends, many of which are the result of the person who first sent out the message not being totally clear in the body of their text.

For example, if they failed to name the author of the piece they're sending out, most often a famous writer who had nothing to do with it is given the credit. The most famous example of this was a piece originally written by a *Chicago Tribune* writer named Mary Schmich. Written as a satirical commencement address to the college graduates of 1997, she insisted that the most important advice she had to give was that they "wear sunscreen." The article was funny and well written and people started sending it to others via email, but the majority of the emails failed to credit Mary Schmich as the author, and it didn't take long for people to assume that it had been a real commencement address. Thanks to the story's amusingly cynical tone and style, people started to credit it to the writer Kurt Vonnegut, who is most famous for his classic 1969 novel *Slaughterhouse-Five*. That should have been that, but the story continued when film director Baz Luhrman, best known for his Academy Award–nominated musical *Moulin Rouge*, read the piece while he was working on a record album entitled *Baz Luhrman Presents*. Luhrman loved the piece enough to want to include it on his record. An Australian voice-over actor named Lee Perry was hired to read it over some spare new-age music, and the result was a huge hit in Australia and a minor hit in America. Had the piece been credited to Mary Schmich all along, it probably would have died out before reaching the famous film director, but because it was erroneously credited to a legendary author it earned itself a strange niche in both journalistic and musical history.

A similar situation led to the legend of the murdered jumper. For seven years it existed in the minds of only a few people, until it was posted on the Internet in August 1994 and became instantly familiar to thousands. Many people were so fascinated by this bizarre story of forensic logic that they sent it to all their friends, often so they could debate the questions raised by the case. In the original post, the parents were not charged and the boy's death was ruled a suicide, but as the story mutated on the Net, every possible legal outcome of the incident was described. In January 1998, the story received its first dramatic recreation on an episode of *Homicide: Life on the Street.* The writers of the show must have been fans of urban legends, as just a month earlier they had dedicated an episode to the legend of the last goodbye, which has already been discussed in this chapter (p. 106). In this case the producers took the interesting step of casting a legendary celebrity couple, Steve Allen and Audrey Meadows, in the roles of the parents whose constant bickering causes the whole confusing tale to take place. A year later, the legend was given its first cinematic treatment at the beginning of director P.T. Anderson's Oscar-nominated film *Magnolia,* which also featured another legend that will be discussed later in this chapter.

So what is the origin of this fascinating legend? It all started in 1987 at a meeting of the American Academy of Forensic Sciences. There a member of the academy named Don Harper Mills told the story to illustrate his point that by changing a few facts in a case you can dramatically affect the charges that result. Mills had mapped out part of the story earlier and invented the other part during the course of his presentation, and he had no idea that some day it would become so well-known.

As complicated as the story is, it still can be solved. The same cannot be said for the mystery of how the story ended up on the Internet seven years after Mills first concocted it. The identity of the person first responsible for posting it on the web is still unknown and likely always will be.

With this new digital age, from now on you should always be aware that whenever you make a story to illustrate a point, you risk the chance that someday you'll end up paying to see it in the latest Tom Cruise movie to hit the multiplex.

A Bug on the Windshield

There was little Willy and his wife, Edina, could do when the government decided to build the highway right next to their home. They tried their best, along with their neighbors, to protest the upcoming project, but the government had already invested too much money into it to be put off by the complaints of a handful of people. They then tried their best to deal with the deafening rumble of the constant traffic, and the litter that spewed out of the cars' speeding windows, but eventually they had enough and tried to sell the house. Unfortunately, they discovered that no one was desperate or stupid enough to purchase a piece of property so close to a busy highway. That left them with just two choices—abandon the house or develop a sense of humor about their horrible situation. In the end they decided they had spent too much money on their home to choose the first option.

So they took to joking about the noise, the litter and the air outside that constantly smelled of exhaust and hot asphalt. To the outside world they started to seem a bit eccentric, but it was the only way they knew to cope. Willy took to burying all the furry creatures he found squashed on the road. After burying each creature he would give it a name, which he would then carve into a piece of wood along with the name of the species and the day he found it, and place it in the ground as a little headstone. Edina took to trying to fight the noise by learning how to play new instruments, each louder than the last. She had mastered the drums, the tuba and was trying her hand at the bagpipes.

One night the two of them were in bed about to go to sleep when they noticed a strange sound they hadn't heard for a while. It was silence. The highway was eerily quiet. They had gotten so used to the constant hum of passing traffic that they found it almost impossible to sleep without it. The silence was so loud it was keeping them awake. Finally, Edina had an idea and turned on their clock radio to a rock station, and the screech of an electric guitar was just noisy enough to do the trick. They both fell asleep.

The radio was still on when they were awakened by the loudest and most painful-sounding crash either had ever heard. They both jumped out of bed and looked out their bedroom window and saw that two semis had driven straight into each other right in front of their house. Edina ran to the phone and called 911, while Willy ran out of the house in his pajamas to see if he could help someone.

It turned out that there was no one to help. Both drivers had been killed in the crash. The police came and found themselves stuck with a serious problem. Both semis had been driving without cargo, so they didn't have to worry about moving two heavy trailers full of goods, but the two trucks had become so wedged together in the crash that they had essentially become one huge obstacle on the road. It was too heavy to tow away, and the only way to transport it safely would be to place it on a flatbed, but a crane—which they did not have—would be needed to get it up there. The best they could do at the moment was move it off to the side of the road by pulling it with a couple of trucks. Willy and Edina, having grown used to the highway's rude impositions, told the police it was perfectly okay to put the wreckage on their front lawn until the police could get the crane they needed to move it.

But because of some miscommunication and a paperwork error, the crane wasn't ordered and the huge, ugly monstrosity was left on Willy and Edina's front lawn for over two months. The unlucky couple tried their best to ignore it, but as the days passed a strange smell began to emanate from the wreckage. Neither of them had smelled anything like it. It made their throats gag and their eyes water whenever they went outside. Eventually it became too much for them, and they started calling the police daily to get them to move the two trucks off their lawn. When that failed, they started calling twice daily, but it was only when they started calling every hour that someone ordered the crane and a crew came over to move the stinking deathtrap away.

Willy and Edina watched the removal from inside their house, which had become possessed by the foul odor, forcing them to go through a can of vanilla-scented aerosol air freshener every day. They felt tremendous relief as they watched the crane lift the wreckage off their lawn, but that relief faded when they heard an ear-splitting squeal. As the wreckage was lifted off the ground, its weight caused it to split apart. The two halves fell to the ground, and the smell exploded across the neighborhood, 10 times stronger than it had been before.

The removal crew dropped to their knees as the stench hit them. They began to gasp and vomit as it overcame them. They crawled into their truck and drove away, leaving Willy and Edina alone to suffer.

A half hour later, two trucks sped onto the lawn filled with men in the kind of white suits professionals wear when dealing with dangerous viruses or nuclear waste. They got out and studied the wreckage with a whole host of strange electronic equipment before they concluded that—as disgusting as it was—the smell wasn't indicative of something hazardous. One of them knocked on Willy and Edina's front door. He kindly handed them two gas masks and explained what they had discovered.

"Turns out the police missed something when they first investigated the accident," the man explained, his voice sounding hollow underneath his mask. "Based on what they found, they assumed that just the two semis had collided, but it turns out that a third vehicle was involved. The best we can figure out, it was one of those small foreign cars. It must have been between the two trucks when it happened. We're not sure yet, but we think there were four people inside it, which explains the smell."

This proved to be the final straw for Willy and Edina. They had no problem with their lawn being a graveyard for animal roadkill, but knowing that it had been home to four dead people was too much for them. They hand painted a sign that read "yours if you want it" and placed it on their front door. Then they packed everything they owned into a trailer and drove away, never to return. And despite their sign, no one ever came to claim their abandoned home.

* * *

There are two possible explanations for the popularity of this legend. The first is that it is a literal interpretation of the phrase "squashed like a bug on a windshield," and the other is that it is subtle jab at the once toy-like quality of many foreign cars. In this age of the SUV, the dichotomy between massive American cars and smaller import cars has become a lot less noticeable, but when this legend first appeared the division was a definite one.

The American auto companies were quick to make fun of the size of the cars manufactured by their international competitors. They even went so far as to suggest that driving an import was unpatriotic and possibly traitorous. This sentiment struck a nerve with many consumers, who accused motorists who bought a car made in Europe or Japan of being un-American. Because of this bias, frequently the subtext of this legend is that the four people whose deaths went unnoticed got what they deserved. If they had been driving a proper car, made in the U.S. of A, they might still have died, but at least the police would have known about it. Their unpleasant fate is a just punishment for choosing affordability and fuel efficiency over supporting their country's economy.

The other explanation is a lot less harsh. One of the most popular of the small import cars was the German Volkswagen Beetle, which was popularly known as "The Bug." With its round curves, its body actually resembled an insect, so the name was apt. The legend, then, could just have been the result of an imaginative storyteller's literal interpretation of the popular phrase mentioned above. A lot of urban legends start out as jokes or deliberately absurd stories, but—as the years pass—the original humorous intent can be lost and the story can end up being presented as fact.

Though many imports can be quite small, it is unlikely to the point of being nearly impossible for an incident like this to really happen, but by now you should know that something as trivial as that isn't enough for the legend to stop being told.

His Father's Boots

Mason had no idea where his father got his boots, but sometimes he wondered if maybe the old guy made a deal with the devil to get them. His father had worn them for close to 15 years, until the day he died. During that time they had been subjected to the worst that the West could offer, having been covered in mud, blood, manure and the occasional glob of chewing tobacco, but when Mason's widowed mother handed them to him they looked little different from when his father had first put them on. To look at them one would never assume that they were that durable, having been crafted in everyday leather without pretensions towards anything but utility. They were comfortable, too.

He wore them for 27 years after his father's death, and even though he put them through even more tortuous conditions than his father had, they still looked only slightly worn and a touch faded. He was wearing them the day he suddenly collapsed after dismounting from his horse. Everyone was caught by surprise as he shouted out with a cry of pain and fell to the ground. By the time his son, Chester, reached him, he was already dead. Everyone assumed he had had a heart attack. After the funeral Chester's mother gave him the boots, knowing that Mason would have wanted him to have them.

Chester didn't put them on right away. He knew how proud his father had been of them and he feared that putting them on so soon after his death would be disrespectful. But after a few months, he felt enough time had passed and he was ready to wear the famously indestructible boots. He was amazed by how comfortable they were, except for an annoying bump at his left big toe.

Only a couple of days later Chester started to feel ill. He complained to his wife that morning that his head hurt and he felt slightly feverish, but that didn't stop him from going out to work the farm. His wife became worried when he didn't come back for lunch that day. She sent their son, Eli, out to look for him. Eli found him sitting on his horse, among a herd of cattle.

"You're worrying Ma," Eli told him when he found him, but Chester didn't say a word back.

As Eli got closer to his father it became clear that something was wrong. When he got right next to him he became frightened by how still he was.

"You okay, Pa?" he asked with a quiver in his voice.

Chester didn't move. Eli grabbed his hand, and he could tell by its eerie chill that his father was dead.

Once again, after just a few months, Chester's mother found herself handing over her late husband's boots. This time they went to Eli, who, at 15, had only just grown big enough to wear them. Like his father he refused to wear them so soon after the funeral. He chose to wait for his 16th birthday before he put them on. He too found them to be just as comfortable as his grandfather and father had, except for the irritating bump under his left big toe.

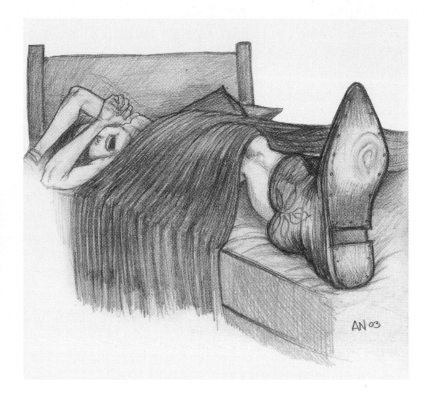

A week passed before one morning he didn't get up for breakfast. His mother shouted at him to get up, but he did not respond. She went in to check on him, and she screamed when she discovered him dead underneath his blankets.

A father and son dying within a couple of months of each other is unusual, yet not out of the question. But a father, son and grandson dying within such a short time is hard to dismiss as mere coincidence. Talk of a curse began to spread among their friends, neighbors and kin, and it was Mason's widow who decided where the curse had come from. She took the decades-old boots—which she herself had handed over from her husband to her son and grandson—and took a knife to them. With a fury she had never felt before she destroyed the boots. It was while she was tearing the left boot apart that she heard the sound of something small and hard fall to the ground. She looked down and picked up the tiny white object.

It was then that she realized that there had been no curse. The death of her loved ones instead had a much more logical explanation, for in her hand she held the tooth of a rattlesnake.

* * *

Since this story takes place in the days of the Wild West, it seems to be a bit of a stretch to call it an urban legend, so let's call this a rural legend instead. The truth is that the story goes back even further than its current western backdrop, having first appeared in print in 1782. This makes it one of the oldest legends in this book, but its longevity is no guarantee of its plausibility.

The reality is that the story simply couldn't happen the way described above. The likelihood of a broken rattlesnake fang carrying enough poison to kill one person, much less two, is very slim. This is especially true since the protruding fang is described as being a bit irritating. For it to be effective the pain would be far closer to excruciating. As described, only the small amount of dry venom at the tip of the tooth would come in contact with Chester and his son, and such a small amount of venom—even over a period of days—wouldn't be nearly enough to kill them. For that to happen the tooth would have to become firmly lodged inside their foot, which—as comfortable as the boots may be—would be something they would both notice right away.

The Deadliest Fizz

Jimmy Torence had every right to be depressed. His parents had disowned him, his girlfriend had dumped him and his latest agent had just told him that he wouldn't be representing him anymore. Still, everyone expected him to smile because he was Little Smiling Jimmy from that cereal commercial that was so ubiquitous in the early 1970s. Jimmy wasn't so little anymore, now that he was 19, but people still recognized him and they always asked him to flash his famous smile. Jimmy hated those people. He didn't feel like smiling, and he resented that people expected him to be nice and friendly just because he had been a cute kid in a commercial over 10 years ago.

He had been able to parlay his initial success into some minor TV and movie roles, but as soon as adolescence reared its ugly head those offers dried up. He wasn't any good in school and wasn't conscientious enough to hold down a regular job, so he made do on the meager income that came from the residual payments he received whenever some desperate cable station played all 13 episodes of the awful sitcom he starred in when he was 11. Those payments, however, were becoming fewer and farther between, and he knew it was only a matter of time before he was forced to get a job as a waiter or security guard. He dreaded what he knew would be the inevitable result of this. People would see him working and he'd see them whisper to each other. "Isn't that Little Smiling Jimmy?" one would ask each the other. "I think it is," the other would respond. "How sad," the first one would shake their head, "he used to be so cute."

Jimmy was sitting alone on his couch when his phone rang. He had no idea who would want to call him, since everyone he could think of wasn't talking to him. He answered the phone and was surprised to hear the voice of an old friend he hadn't seen in four years. Tony had been a fellow child actor. He had played the role of Jimmy's older brother in that awful sitcom, and his post-adolescent acting career had stalled just as badly as Jimmy's had.

"What's up, Jimmy?"

"Not much. How you doing, Tony?"

"I'm doing great, man!"

"That's good. What have you been up to?"

"I went to film school in New York."

"Really?"

"Yeah. That's why I'm calling. I got this gig directing this cheesy horror movie and I wanted to know if you were available to play a part in it."

Jimmy sat straight up on his couch.

"You want to give me a part in a movie?" he asked incredulously.

"You bet. It's going to be a direct-to-video ultra low-budget sort of deal, but I'm planning some stuff that should make it memorable."

"What's the part?"

"The lead's wacky sidekick. It's a funny part."

"Why me?"

"My producer wants a few names in the cast, but we have no money in the budget to afford them, so I thought maybe my old pal would be willing to help me out. How about it?"

Jimmy didn't have to think about it.

"I'll do it!"

They had only a week to shoot the whole movie, so it went by pretty fast, but it was easily the best week of Jimmy's life. He got along great with his cast mates and the crew and had a ball playing the hero's wacky sidekick who ends up getting devoured by a gang of zombified cannibalistic cheerleaders. He didn't want the shoot to end, so when it wrapped he felt a little depressed, afraid that it meant a return to his current misery. He tried his best to hide his sadness at the cast and crew party that Tony threw at his house the next week.

Tony was the type of guy who threw a party only if he could think of a theme for it. The theme of this party was "A Return to Childhood," and Tony had gone all out to make it happen. He had everyone play Pin the Tail on the Donkey, he made them dance the Hokey-Pokey and for refreshments he supplied a dizzying array of candy, cake and soda pop.

Despite his concerns about the bleakness of his future, Jimmy still managed to have a good time at the party. He had to admit that if he were 9 or 10 again, this would have been the all-time best party ever. At 19 it was still a lot of fun.

While a Chipmunks album played in the background and Tony started to organize a game of tag to play outside, Jimmy got up and took a look at all the candy that lined the long table at the back of the living room. He grabbed a can of cola and sipped from it while he looked for some new candy to try. In a large bowl he saw a purple crystal-like candy he had never seen before. He grabbed a small piece and popped it into his mouth. It was grape-flavored and to his surprise it popped and fizzed inside his mouth. The sensation was oddly pleasurable.

He grabbed a large handful of the small candies and threw them into his mouth. They felt like little candy landmines as they exploded on his tongue. As they popped and fizzed he took a long drink from his pop to wash them down.

He turned around and saw that everyone was going outside to play tag and he started to move to join them, but as he did a tremendous pain suddenly hit him in his stomach. It was so excruciating he cried out and fell to the floor. Everyone turned around and watched as he struggled on the ground. Tony ran to his phone and called 911 for an ambulance, but the paramedics were too late. Jimmy was dead by the time that they got there.

During his autopsy it was determined that his stomach had burst open as a result of a tremendous buildup of carbon dioxide, caused by the combination of the carbonated candy and the carbonated soft drink.

Word quickly spread that Little Smiling Jimmy had died from eating Pop Rocks—which was what the candy was called—and drinking pop at the same time. It was because of this that many lives were spared, as others now knew not to make his same mistake.

* * *

As we've seen in other legends in this book, one of the best ways to make an absurd urban legend more believable and evocative is to attach it to a famous personality. In the case of this particular legend the victim is most often said to be "Mikey," the young kid whose famed commercial for Life cereal played for years and years during the late 1970s and early '80s. He was a very effective person to place in the story because, on the one hand, everyone in the English-speaking world knew who he was, while on the other hand, no one knew his real name or anything else about him that would prove the story to be false.

The truth is that John Gilchrist, who played Mikey, is still very much alive and works in the advertising department of a New York radio station. As for the idea that combining Pop Rocks and soda pop can kill you, there is one easy way to disprove it. Taking my life in my hands, I decided—in the best interests of this book—to try it myself. No longer marketed as Pop Rocks, the fizzy candy can still be found on store shelves under a different name. I purchased some, along with a bottle of cola, and combined them inside my mouth. The result was very messy (some of the fizz dribbled down my chin) but I survived to tell the tale.

Like the story about spider legs and webs being used to manufacture Bubble Yum bubblegum, this legend most likely got its start on some playground where a group of kids were marveling over the effects of the fizzy candy. A few speculations on their part about what could happen when the candy was combined with soda pop, and voila, a legend was born.

The legend was further aided by the fact that Pop Rocks disappeared from shelves in 1983, but that was because the rights to market the candy were bought from General Mills by Kraft Foods, which marketed it under a different name. The name has changed several times since then, but the little fizzy candies have been available everywhere ever since.

How'd She Get up There?

A husband and wife pair of forest rangers, June and Henry, were close to tears as they inspected the damage wrought by the fire that had raged throughout their domain for two weeks. The fire crews had managed to put it out a week before, but only now was the forest safe enough to walk through. But as they walked, the two of them quickly concluded that the word "forest" was now pathetically inappropriate. Its once-mighty trees had been reduced to lifeless black skeletons and piles of heavy ash. There were no animals in sight; the smell of cooked flesh indicated where many of them had gone.

The experience was proving too much for June, who was so overwhelmed by the destruction around her that she began to feel ill. A wave of nausea swept over her and she ran over to a nearby tree to throw up. She coughed and cried after it was over. Henry walked over to her and patted her back and told her that it was going to be okay. He handed her a handkerchief and she used it to clean up her face. When she was done he gave her a long hug. It was while they stood embracing that he saw it.

"What is that?" he asked aloud.

June broke the hug and turned around.

"What?" she asked him.

"Over there," he said as he pointed.

June followed his finger with her eyes and caught sight of a strange figure aloft in the limbs of a blackened tree. Although it too was burnt, she recognized the shape. It took her a moment for her brain to believe her eyes, as it was a shape that had no business being where it was.

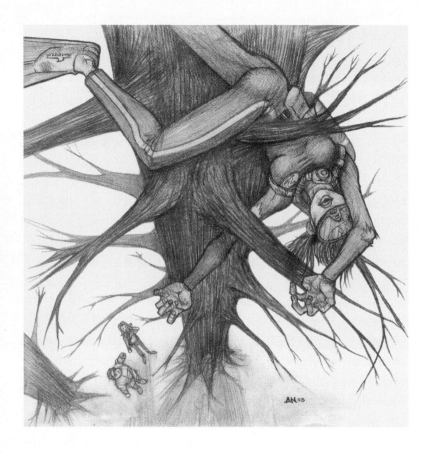

"That's..." she paused, not quite sure if she really believed it, "that's a scuba diver."

Henry breathed out gratefully, happy to hear that she saw the same thing. When he had first seen it he had thought his despair had affected his mind, but it hadn't. Up in the tree there really sat the burnt remains of a person in full self-contained underwater breathing apparatus regalia.

The police were brought in to investigate. It took some time to get the body down, as the fire damage made the tree unstable. To pass the time one detective told the others a story about a case he had heard about that was even stranger than this one.

"—So the kid ended up being noted as an accomplice to his own murder. What are the chances, huh? Too bad he died. A guy with that kind of strange luck would have been a shoo-in to win the lottery."

When they finally got the body down, they discovered that the burns it suffered were superficial and were not the cause of death. The wetsuit and much of the other equipment had melted and it took some time to remove the mask and get a look at the person's face. When they finally got it all off they saw that it was a young woman.

Her name was Iris Mathers. Five days earlier an aquatic search party had been formed at the lake where she had last dived, after she had failed to come back up. The lake was over 200 miles away from the forest. The storytelling detective noted the puzzled look on his partner's face.

"Don't worry about it," he smiled, "all we have to do is figure out how she got from the bottom of a lake to the top of a burning tree a couple of hundred miles away. No problem. We'll have it all figured out by lunch tomorrow. And if I'm wrong, I'm buying."

The detective didn't have to pay for lunch that next day. As bizarre as it seemed, the explanation for what happened turned out to be rather simple. As part of the firefighting effort, helicopters were used to dump water over the burning forest. To do this they used large contraptions known as "bambi buckets," which were filled by being lowered into nearby bodies of water. Poor Iris had chosen the wrong day and the wrong lake to go diving in. As she was in the water she had been lifted up into one of these buckets. She must have been very confused as she felt herself rise up into the air, and she must have been horrified when the bucket emptied and she felt herself fall towards the blazing heat of the burning fire. Her terror, it turned out, was what had killed her. She was dead before she landed in the tree, having died of a heart attack caused by the shock of her situation.

* * *

Just like the story of the murdered jumper, many people first heard about the legend of the out-of-place scuba diver when they saw it at the beginning of writer-director P.T. Anderson's film *Magnolia*. In the film the legend was depicted as fact, with the added twist that the scuba diver was also a blackjack dealer at a Nevada casino and the man who flew the plane that lifted him out of the water was an addicted gambler who had lost big to the diver just the night before. Though this detail adds an interesting note of off-putting coincidence to the story, it isn't a part of the original legend, in which the pilot of the plane is seldom mentioned.

This story has a lot in common with the murdered jumper legend, in that both got their start as intellectual puzzles. They both depict bizarre hard-to-explain deaths, and what makes them fun is trying to figure out how they happened. However, unlike the other legend, the solution most often given to this puzzle is flawed to the point of being impossible. There is simply no way that the scuba diver in the story could get into the tree in the manner that is described.

The story makes reference to "bambi buckets," the large devices used to carry water over forest fires by helicopters.

The largest of these buckets can easily hold 10,000 gallons of water, which is more than big enough to carry a person, but—no matter the size of the bucket—they all have the same aperture size with which to take in the water—1 foot. That is not nearly large enough for a person to fit through. There is no way a person could be picked up by one of these buckets. In reality Iris most likely would have been hit by the heavy bucket and either have been killed instantly or knocked unconscious long enough to drown, rather than be hoisted up into the air.

Bombardier airplanes are also used to fight fires. They fill their large tanks by flying over bodies of water, but their intakes are even smaller than the ones on the buckets used by helicopters. To make the legend even more impossible, grills through which no person could pass cover these intakes.

Over the years this legend has become the bane of professional divers, who have grown tired of explaining why it couldn't happen. A few, however, have used the legend to have some fun on the Internet. There they created a website, www.firediving.com, with which they try to convince the gullible that not only do scuba divers get picked up in this manner all the time, but that they do it deliberately as part of one of the world's most extreme sports. It would be interesting to find out how many people who have visited the site didn't realize that it was a joke.

What sets this legend apart isn't that the situation it describes is impossible, but its explanation of the situation is impossible. There is no reason a scuba diver couldn't be found up in a tree after a forest fire, but how he or she got up there would require a much different explanation.

5
Multiple Maniacs

*N*ow this is what you were waiting for, right? Some sick tales of murderous psychopaths carving a bloody path through the populace at large. But have you ever considered what the world would be like if every legend involving one of these maniacs was true? Considering the body count numbers these guys rack up, there wouldn't be anybody left to tell their stories after they were finished.

As frightening as these legends may seem, take heart in the fact that not a single one of them really happened. As I stated before in my introduction, if there is one moral to be learned while reading this book it is that the world is safer than we imagine. Yes, dangerous people exist and one must always be wary around strangers, but that does not mean you should allow stories like the eight you're about to read convince you that everywhere you go a beautiful stranger is waiting to steal your kidneys, a gang member is going to slash your ankles or a bunch of teenagers are going to throw a makeshift bomb into your car. Chances are, at most, only one of these things will happen to you during your lifetime, so you need not fear the other two.

Way Out of His League

Donald Speckler was a sales representative for a company that made bath towels for hotel chains. Part of his job required him to travel all over the country and stay at every hotel his company sold to. This meant he was away from home for close to six months out of the year, which made it very hard for him to have a serious relationship. He had tried answering personal ads and speed dating, but, even though he made a good living and owned a nice car, he wasn't what most women look for in a man. He was short and bald and chubby. He tried his best to wear nice clothes, but they never looked right on him and he found it impossible to not spill food on them. He snored loudly and no matter how much mouthwash he gargled he always had bad breath. But despite these annoying habits he was also a nice man who enjoyed listening to people. The problem was that there were very few women who were willing to take the time to get to know him and find that out.

He had been traveling all through Florida for two weeks and was now in Miami. The hot weather made him sweat profusely, and no matter how much he showered and used deodorant he was never able to completely mask the smell of his BO. Still, he didn't let this deter him from going downstairs to spend some time in the hotel's lounge.

Throughout his travels Donald had spent a lot of time in lounges all across America, and this was easily one of the nicest he had ever seen. It was dark and tasteful and its patrons were all attractive and well dressed. For a moment Donald was taken aback by the glamour of the room. He couldn't think of the last time he had seen so many beautiful women in one place. He walked over to the bar and sat down on one of its stools. He ordered a beer and turned around to get another look at what the room had to offer. Just then his eyes caught sight of a gorgeous blonde sitting alone in a booth to his right. Donald, despite the cruelties inflicted on him by his own body, liked to think of himself as somewhat sophisticated, but looking at the woman made him feel like a small town rube catching his first glimpse of the big city. She looked just like a movie star or a supermodel.

He tried his best to look away from her, not wanting to be caught staring at her, but his eyes refused to listen to his brain and they kept moving back to her, where they basked in her radiant glow. He knew it was only a matter of time before she would catch him, but he couldn't help himself. He just hoped she didn't have a huge boyfriend who'd pound him into confetti for ogling his girlfriend. It was because of this reasonable paranoia that the way she reacted when she did catch him looking at her caught him totally by surprise. Donald couldn't believe it when he saw it, but—instead of glaring at him or pointing her index finger towards her mouth to mime the act of throwing up—she smiled at him and used her index finger to tell him to come over and sit beside her.

Donald looked at his beer to make sure that he hadn't accidentally been given something much stronger, but when he looked back up he saw that the woman was still smiling at him. Hesitantly, he pointed to himself to make sure that he was the one she was smiling at. She laughed and nodded and before she could change her mind Donald jumped off his seat and sat down right beside her.

"Hi, I'm Donald," he said as he sat down.

"I'm Jennifer," she grinned at him, her voice managing the difficult trick of sounding both sultry and friendly at the same time. "I couldn't help but notice you sitting over there."

"Yeah, I'm sorry. I didn't mean to stare like that. I'm usually not that rude."

"That's okay. I was flattered."

"I suppose you're waiting for somebody, huh?"

"Nope," Jennifer shook her head. "I don't know anyone in Miami. I'm here on business."

"Really? Me too."

"What do you do?"

"I sell towels to hotels. You?"

"I deal in hospital supplies."

For the next three hours the two of them sat in the booth and drank and laughed together. Donald could not get over his good fortune. Here was a smart, funny woman who knew exactly what his life was like. After a while he had forgotten how beautiful she was and had become seriously enamored with the person she was inside. It was because of this he made a move that for him was unusually bold.

"It's getting late, Jennifer," he said as he nervously rubbed his thumb against the rim of his glass, "and since we both have to be up early tomorrow I was wondering if—"

"—I'd love to," she interrupted him.

"Really?"

She smiled and nodded, and he tried to look nonchalant while his heart pounded a million miles per hour in his chest. As coolly as he could he took out his wallet and took out enough money to pay for their drinks, along with a generous tip, and the two of them got out of the booth and walked out of the lounge.

Before they got to his hotel room, Jennifer asked to stop at hers. She went in for a minute and came back out with a bottle of champagne. "I got this in a gift basket a doctor sent me because I got him a good deal," she said.

Feeling a combination of nervous anticipation and tremendous elation, Donald fumbled with his key card as he tried to open his door. When he finally managed to success-fully open the door he laughed and sang out a flat "ta-da!" as he motioned for her to go inside. Jennifer looked festive as she popped open the champagne while he turned on the light. Bubbly spilled out messily onto the carpet and they both laughed at the spontaneity of the experience. Donald went over to the mini-bar and found two plastic glasses. Jennifer poured some champagne into both of them and they toasted each other before they took a drink.

The first thing Donald noticed when he woke up was that he had a headache and he was unusually cold. His eyesight was blurred and he had to squint to make out his surround-ings. He was surprised to find that he was in his hotel's bath-tub. He tried to move and felt a sharp jolt of pain through his right side. He looked down and was shocked to discover that he was covered in ice. He tried to move again, and this time he felt a needle move in his left arm. He looked up and saw that he was connected to a hospital I.V. Taped to the metal stand was a handwritten note.

Dear Donald,
I said I dealt in hospital supplies, didn't I? If I were you I would get out of the tub very slowly and call 911 right now. Tell them that someone has taken one of your kidneys. The ambulance

should come and pick you up right away. Don't worry, you should be fine, and maybe next time you'll be a little more careful about who you stare at when you're in a bar.

Thanks,
Jennifer

* * *

The preceding story is an example of not one, but two, classic fixtures of urban legend lore—the beautiful stranger and the stolen organ. These story elements appear in many different legends, but are most often told together. In other versions of the stolen organ legend, groups of armed men kidnap tourists in foreign countries and cut out whatever is currently selling on the black market, or hospitals find the organs they need for rich customers by taking them from homeless people. The most well-known alternate version of the beautiful stranger legend is the one in which the victim takes the woman who is obviously out of his league back to his hotel room and actually becomes intimate with her, but when he wakes up he finds that she has gone and left a message for him on his bathroom mirror written in red lipstick. It reads "Welcome to the wonderful world of AIDS."

The idea that people would be so desperate for life-saving transplants that they would be willing to buy organs from the black market without any regard for where they may have came from isn't hard to swallow. In a world where people have actually tried to sell one of their kidneys online, it isn't too hard to believe that somewhere out there, there is an enterprising person willing to take unusual steps to meet the demand. The problem is that, as the legend is told, it just isn't medically possible. Removing a living person's kidney is such a complicated procedure it would be impossible for someone to perform the operation alone in a person's hotel room. Even if you allow that the woman in the story had help, and the victim was moved to another location for the operation, it still defies all notions of medical logic. The amount of blood Donald would have lost from the type of cut required would easily cause him to bleed to death before he woke up in the morning. Plus, there is a reason donated kidneys most often come from patients' relatives, as they are less likely to be rejected. A kidney donated by a stranger is much more likely to cause problems and would therefore be undesirable from a medical standpoint.

Still, of all the urban legends in this book, this was the one most people told me they believed. This may be because the different versions of the legend have been referenced in several TV shows and movies over the years, giving it a patina of reality. In one case in 1994, people's willingness to believe the legend almost resulted in a woman being killed by a mob.

During that time the citizens of Guatemala had come to believe that North American and European tourists were coming to their country for the direct purpose of abducting babies and stealing their organs. On March 29 of that year this mistrust of tourists came to a head when two Guatemalan patrollers accused an American woman of kidnapping a small boy so she could steal his organs. Before she could protest, the 51-year-old environmental activist from Alaska was dragged out of her bus by an enraged mob that beat her so badly they broke her arms and left her with internal injuries so severe that she was in a coma for over a month.

Bet you never thought that an urban legend could be so dangerous, did you?

Just Another Scream in the Night

Sara couldn't wait for midnight. She remembered how fun it had been last year, with everyone coming together and getting their frustrations out in a moment of shared catharsis. Until then she stared at the philosophy textbook in front of her. She had been reading it for so long now that it no longer made any sense to her. Each sentence seemed like gibberish to her and it took all her concentration to translate it into a form of English she could understand.

"I'm so going to fail," she sighed to her roommate Kathy, who was fighting her own battle with a biology textbook.

"Don't worry," Kathy muttered distractedly without looking up, "you'll do fine."

"But I don't get any of this! I keep reading the same chapter over and over again and it still seems like the same load of bull each time."

Kathy finally looked up.

"All you're doing is psyching yourself out. I've heard you talking to guys at parties about this stuff and you sounded like you knew what you were talking about."

"I was just dropping names and pretending I knew what they wrote about," Sara admitted.

"Well, you fooled me," said Kathy, "and who knows? You may get lucky."

"How do you mean?"

"I have this friend who knew this guy who opened up his philosophy test book and the only question on it was 'why?'"

"That's not true…" Sara replied.

"No, this really happened. It was the only question and he had no idea how he was supposed to answer it, so he just wrote down 'why not?' and handed it in."

"So, he failed. Way to pep me up, Kathy."

"But that's just it. He didn't fail. All the other students wrote these long pretentious essays, but the prof was looking for the clearest and most concise answer possible. The guy got the only A in the class. So all you have to do is try to answer everything as simply as you can. Don't get too complicated and you'll be fine."

Sara wasn't convinced, but she stayed quiet.

"What time is it?" asked Kathy.

"11:30," Sara noted, checking her alarm clock.

"Just another half hour. I can't wait." Kathy put down her book. "I'm going to grab a coffee before it happens. Wanna come?"

"No, I've got to try to read this chapter one more time before it gets crazy."

"Okay."

Kathy walked out of their dorm room and left Sara alone to study. As she stared at the words this time, something strange started to happen. They started to make sense. She felt a surge of exhilaration flow through her as her mind started to make all the connections it hadn't been able to make before. The process was so exhilarating that she lost track of time, and when she finally looked over at her alarm clock it read 11:56. For a second she considered skipping the event she had spent the whole night looking forward to, but she decided that she wasn't going to lose her newfound insight if she took a break for 10 minutes or so. She got up and walked out of her dorm room and

started heading towards the quad, where all the students had started to gather.

It was a warm night and the full moon shone brightly in the clear sky. The quad was a fair distance away so she started to half-jog towards it, but even then she started to hear the screams that indicated that it had begun.

Every year on the last Sunday before exams it was traditional for the students to come together and scream until their throats were hoarse and their fears of failure and the lifetime of poverty and destitution that would result were eased by the adrenaline pumping through their systems.

Sara turned her half-jog into a run as she tried to get to the quad before the ceremony ended. As she ran she decided to take a detour off the well-lit path and take a shortcut through a swath of trees to her right. As she ran into the small wooded area towards the quad, she was suddenly cut short by a heavy and painful blow to her midsection. She fell to the ground and looked up to see a large man with a black ski mask over his face. She was horrified to see that in his hand was a very large butcher knife.

"I hoped someone like you would come along," he told her before he rose up the knife, "I waited here last year and no one showed up."

Sara screamed and screamed, but no one heard her. Her cries for help were lost in the cacophony coming from the quad. The man in the ski mask brought down the knife and Sara's screams ceased, just as the ones coming from the other side of the trees started to die out.

* * *

Legends like this one are usually the hardest to disprove as the individual elements are not unrealistic or illogical. The fact is that over the years ceremonies like the one described here have occurred at campuses throughout North America. It is also true that on those same campuses women have been attacked and/or killed by violent predators. But there is no record at any school of these two things happening at the same time.

There are two good explanations for the origin of this legend. The first is that it came from students who disapproved of the practice, because it interrupted their sleep or because of more ideological reasons. The other is that it is meant to be a metaphor for the way society so frequently ignores the problem of violence against women. For Sara screams and screams, but is not heard.

In this way the story is reminiscent of a real-life incident that occurred in Queens, New York, in 1964. In this famous case, the cries of the victim, a woman named Kitty Genovese, were heard by her neighbors as she was attacked and killed, but they were ignored. While the students so close to Sara could be forgiven for not hearing her pleas over the din, these men and women ignored Kitty's cries because they didn't want to get involved. This makes for the strange case of a legend being far less disturbing than the reality.

All the Kids Are Doing It!

Norm was not the kind of guy to rock the boat. The poster boy for peer pressure, he never questioned the activities that his friends took part in, no matter how dangerous or destructive they were. When they went to graveyards to steal gravestones and smash monuments, he was right there with them taking chunks out of a two-year-old child's grave with a sledgehammer. When they went down streets and slashed the tires of parked cars, he flattened as many as they did. Perhaps his willingness to join in wouldn't have been so problematic if he was involved with a less-psychotic group of friends, but since they all seemed to take some pleasure in causing the suffering of others, so did he.

It was only by luck that he had never gotten in trouble. He and his friends had managed to never get caught, so their parents had no idea what they did at night. If they had, chances are they never would have allowed the kids to get together, as they all came from fine upstanding, middle-class families where rules were respected and civility was prized above all. Judy and Martin, Norm's parents, sincerely believed that he was a good kid who did well in school and who was above the kind of stunts that so many other kids ruined their lives with. But a person can be lucky for only so long, and it was inevitable that one day this illusion would be shattered.

It was a Friday night and Norm and his friends were bored out of their minds. They were sitting in Gene's basement trying to think of something to do when Vincent came running downstairs with a box in his hands.

"Guys," he spoke to them excitedly, "I just heard about this cool new game they're playing in the city. It's called

Spunkball. My cousin told me all about it. He said they play it all the time."

"How do you play it?" asked Peter.

Vincent dropped the box on the coffee table and rummaged through its contents.

"What you do is you take a rag," he lifted a small piece of red cloth out of the box, "and you pour some gasoline or lighter fluid on it." He grabbed a canister of lighter fluid and squirted the flammable liquid onto the rag. "Then you wrap it in tinfoil." He grabbed a handful of foil and sculpted it into a ball surrounding the rag. "Then you tape a firecracker to it, and voila! A spunkball."

"What do you do with it?" asked Norm.

"You drive around until you see a car with an open window and then you light the firecracker and throw it into the car."

"What happens then?" asked Gene.

"The firecracker explodes and causes the tinfoil to shred and the rag starts on fire," Vincent laughed. His friends joined in, as they thought this was hilarious.

"Well, what are we waiting for?" asked Peter. "Let's play!"

With that the four of them ran out of the basement with Vincent's box and into his car. As they drove around, Peter and Gene sat in the back and sculpted the spunkballs while Norm and Vincent searched for viable targets.

"There's one!" Norm pointed when he saw a parked car with an open window.

"Is anyone in it?" asked Vincent.

"I don't think so."

"Then it's worth 5 points. You get 10 if there is one person in the car, 20 if there's two and 40 if the car is full," he explained to them as he turn the car so Norm could throw their first ball, which Peter had just handed to him. He drove slowly past the parked car and Norm lit the firecracker and threw the spunkball into the window. They laughed and cheered when the firecracker exploded, and a fire started in the car as they drove away.

"Five points for Norm," Vincent laughed, "you guys think you can beat him?"

"No problem," grinned Peter.

"Easily," insisted Gene, "but we gotta get out of the suburbs first."

"You want to drive to the city?" asked Vincent.

"Yeah, there's more people there and we're less likely to get recognized."

His logic made sense to everyone, so Vincent drove out of their quiet little community and started the 45-minute drive towards the city. During that time Peter and Gene used up all the material that Vincent had brought and put together seven more spunkballs, which gave them two shots each (including the one Norm had already taken). The guy with the most points after those two shots would be the winner.

They'd been in the city for only two minutes when Gene decided to take a shot at a passing truck that contained a lone male driver. He lit the firecracker and lobbed it into the truck's open window. They laughed and high-fived each other when the firecracker exploded and the truck swerved behind them as the shocked driver tried to put the fire out.

"Ten points for Gene, five points for Norm," tallied Vincent.

It took 15 minutes for Peter to find a good shot, but he blew it when the car sped up suddenly and the spunkball bounced off the car's closed back window and fell onto the street.

"Deflected!" The other three shouted out in unison as the spunkball exploded on the street.

"Peter fails to score," announced Vincent. "Now somebody else has to drive so I can have a turn."

He parked the car and Norm switched places with Vincent. Vincent waited for 20 minutes before he took a shot at a car that contained two kids their age on a date. His spunkball managed to make it in, but the firecracker on it turned out to be a dud and just fizzled out without exploding.

"How do we score that?" asked Norm. They thought about it and eventually agreed after some debate that all that mattered was that the spunkball made it into the car, and that what it did after that was just gravy.

"So that puts me into the lead with 20," said Vincent. "Time for your second shot, Norm."

"Why don't we skip me so I'm last? That way we only have to switch places one more time."

"Okay," Vincent agreed, "that puts you up next, Gene."

Five minutes later Gene moved ahead of Vincent on the scoreboard with a well-executed 20 pointer. The two older men in the car he scored from nearly crashed into a light post as they tried to deal with the fire.

Peter finally made it onto the board with a 10 pointer.

"You can't win 'em all," Vincent told him as he grabbed a spunkball for his turn. He had to wait 10 minutes before he was able to take his last shot. It was another 20 pointer, and this time the spunkball exploded the way it was supposed to. They turned around and watched as the car screeched to a sudden halt and was rear-ended by the car right behind it. Despite Vincent's protests, they decided that the accident wasn't worth bonus points.

Norm stopped the car and he and Vincent switched again so he could take his last turn. Norm wanted to win and that meant having to find a car with four people in it. The other three jeered and booed him as he passed up several opportunities while he waited for a game-winning shot. Finally after a half hour he saw his chance and threw the lit spunkball into a black sedan that contained four middle-aged women. This time the car in question failed to miss the light post as it swerved and crashed deafeningly behind them. The four of them cheered and Norm started singing "I Am the Champion" in a loud and obnoxious voice.

Out of spunkballs, they drove around the city for another two hours before they headed back home. Vincent dropped Norm off at his house, which he was surprised to find was empty. He checked the answering machine and saw that it had a message on it. He hit the play button and listened to the voice of his father.

"Norm," he said, "I'm at St. Joseph's Hospital. Your mom went down to the city to see a movie with some friends and they had an accident. Call my cell as soon as you hear this."

Norm grabbed the phone and called his dad.

"Is she okay?" he asked his dad as soon as he answered.

"She's in critical," his dad sighed wearily. "The doctor's say it's too soon to tell how she's going to do."

"What happened?"

"Something caused Mrs. Denver to swerve suddenly and drive the car into a light post. She and Mrs. Johnston were killed in the impact. Your mom and Mrs. Reynolds managed to survive the crash, but your mom went into a coma as soon as the medics arrived."

"And Mrs. Reynolds?"

"She escaped with just a broken arm. She says that the accident happened because somebody threw a bomb into the car. She's told the police what kind of car it was and she gave them part of its license plate number, so hopefully the bastards who did this are going to spend a long time in jail." Norm's dad waited for his son to say something, but all he heard was silence.

"Norm? Are you still there? Is something wrong?"

* * *

This creepy tale of juvenile delinquency comes to us directly from our society's all-consuming fear of its own teenagers. Thanks to the inevitable differences between the generations, adults are always convinced that somewhere out there a young person is ready, willing and waiting to do something horrible to them. It is mainly because of urban legends such as this one that people insist that the kids today are out of control and lack any sense of morality, when the reality is that the number of violent crimes caused by teenagers hasn't changed significantly since the 1950s.

That is not to say that there haven't been cases of sociopathic kids killing innocent bystanders in the name of "fun," but the truth is that these incidents do not happen with the frequency legends like this ask you to believe. Spunkball has never been the popular craze the legend depicts it as. In fact, there is no evidence it has ever really been played at all.

The story is also more than just a warning about the dangers of bored, unsupervised kids. It's also a morality tale about the dangers of peer pressure that has all the subtlety of a 1980s' *After School Special,* as Norm suffers tragically because of his willingness to unquestionably follow his friends as they go about causing mayhem. The paradox is that the legend is both positive and negative. It's positive in that it tells kids to stand up for themselves and not break the law just because their friends do, but it's also negative because it depends on a hurtful and unfair generational stereotype to get that message across. No one said these legends weren't complex.

The Letter Home

Mrs. Kleinhorne hadn't gotten a letter from her son Carl for over six months, and the worry was starting to affect her mind. When he first shipped out to Vietnam he had faithfully sent her a letter every week. His letters were always sweet and reassuring, as he was sent there to serve as a file clerk and had thus far avoided any combat, but then they had just stopped coming. It was if he had vanished from the face of the Earth. She tried to get some information from the army, but the officials couldn't tell her what had happened to him.

As the days passed she refused to accept that the worse might have happened. She watched the news every day and knew all about the horrible things that were happening over there, but she couldn't let herself believe that something like that may have happened to Carl. Her body began to grow frail as her lack of appetite started to take its toll. She went to a doctor and he gave her some pills to help ease her anxiety, but she stopped taking them when she once woke up and saw a man who looked like Carl standing above her in her bedroom. He was screaming and crying, and though he faded from sight almost immediately, she could tell that there was something missing from his body.

But then, just as she was about to succumb to her despair, a letter came. She wept as she held it and opened it, as all her worst fears ebbed out of her mind. Like all his letters, it was typewritten, but it was much shorter than the others. It read:

Dear Mom,

I'm sorry it has been so long since I have written, but six months ago I was captured by enemy troops during a trip to the front with my commander. Please don't worry, as though they are our enemy they have treated us very well. I am fed every day and my cell is warm. They say that I will be freed when the war ends, so I will see you then.

Love,
Carl

P.S. Make sure you steam off the stamp on the envelope, so you can give it to young Frankie.

As horrible as it was to find out that Carl was a prisoner of war, it was still a great relief to find out that he was alive and being treated well. She read the letter 20 times, and each time she did she became confused by the letter's postscript. She had no idea who Carl meant by "young Frankie." She tried to think of the names of all his friends and couldn't think of a single Frankie, Frank or Franklin. It was such a strange request that she couldn't help wondering if it was some sort of hidden message.

She decided that the best thing to do was do as he asked and steam off the stamp on the envelope, so she went into the kitchen and put her kettle on. Minutes later she held the envelope over the whistling steam, and the glue on the stamp lost its tack. She lifted it up and saw something so horrifying her heart almost stopped. There in the space where the stamp had been, in a hard to decipher scrawl, was a short handwritten message. It read:

They cut off my hands.

* * *

As a ghoulish anecdote about the brutality of war, the legend of the letter home is particularly chilling, but as a story it's simply too illogical to be believed. The main question the tale begs is how exactly did Carl type the letter? While it is possible that he dictated it to an enemy soldier at the camp, how then did he get the opportunity to write his secret message? And how did he write the message if he had no hands? While it may be possible for someone who has grown up and spent their entire life without their hands to be able to write with a pen in their mouth or between their toes, someone who had only recently been forced to learn the skill would not be able to write the message small enough so it could be hidden by the stamp.

The letter home isn't the only urban legend that deals with prisoners of war. One of the most well-known is the one about Jane Fonda and her visit to the POWs in Hanoi. In this story the prisoners are lined up so the actress can inspect them, and as she goes down the line she shakes their hands and calls them murderers and baby killers. Assuming that this is just an act and that she is really there to help, the prisoners slip her messages to their families and to military officials. But, instead of pocketing the slips of paper, Jane is said to give them to the camp's commander in front of the prisoners, proving whose side she is really on. The commander of the camp then punishes the prisoners for their attempt to contact the outside world, and several of them die in the process.

While the actress really did visit the American prisoners being held in Hanoi, the legend of her betrayal is just that—a legend. Even though the men who were held prisoner at the infamous "Hanoi Hilton" were disgusted by her visit and took it as an unforgivable slap in the face, none of them ever suggested that her visit led to the deaths of some of their comrades. Her visit may have been in bad taste and highly unpatriotic, but it wasn't evil.

In the end these stories are little more than propaganda. Their main purpose is to show the public just why wars such as Vietnam have to be fought. The enemy, the legends insist, are far more barbarous than we are and so we are doomed if they win. This urban legend suggests that an urban legend can be more than just a funny or scary story; it can also be a political tool.

Her First and Only Starring Role

All her life Lizette had dreamed of becoming a famous Hollywood star. Ever since her mother first plopped her down in front of the TV set, she had wanted to become a part of the world that she saw projected on its screen. Luckily for her, her dream wasn't completely out of reach, as nature was kind to her and blessed her with the kind of fresh good looks that were so important to people who were famous and untalented. Her hair was long and blonde, her smile was wide and her blue eyes didn't betray any evidence of an interior monologue inside her mind, so she was perfect for the kind of job that involved pointing to cars on game shows or interviewing rock stars on music video stations.

But, unfortunately, there were many other young men and women in Hollywood who were just as perfect as she was, and many of them had the contacts she lacked to get these coveted jobs, so she was forced to make do as a hostess at an unpopular steakhouse in the valley.

When she moved to L.A. she had assumed that she'd be working full-time on television within four months, but it had taken her a year and a half just to sign up with the city's least-impressive talent agency. After that she was lucky to get an audition every three months or so, and so far she hadn't gotten a single callback, much less an actual job. In the meantime she spent most of her steakhouse money on acting classes taught by guys whose biggest claim to fame was playing the wacky neighbor for half a season on a sitcom in 1984. What little she had left over was being saved for a nose job one casting director suggested she get when she auditioned for the role of Third Streetwalker in an episode of a syndicated cop show.

As depressing as her situation was, she never lost faith that someday she would get that all important life-changing job and she would shoot straight up the ladder of success and become the world-famous celebrity she knew she was destined to be. She knew that all she had to be was patient.

Two and a half years into her wait, she got home one night after a particularly horrible shift at the steakhouse and found that her agent, Joey, had left a message for her on her machine. As far as agents went, Joey was pretty much the bottom of the barrel, but he was still better than no agent at all. Cursed with myriad allergies, he always sounded as if he had a cold and he sniffed and sniveled his way throughout the message.

"Hi, Lizette," he coughed, "it's me, Joey. I just got off the phone with these guys who are doing a low-budget indie flick, and, based on your headshot, they think you're perfect for the lead. Call me back right away and we'll set up a meeting."

Lizette nearly broke her index finger she dialed Joey's number so fast.

"'Ello?" he answered.

"They want to give me the lead?" she asked right away, too excited to exchange greetings.

"Oh, hi Lizette," Joey sniveled, "yeah. They think you're the one."

"What kind of movie is it?"

"Sounds like some sort of thriller. You know, one of those serial killer things."

"And who would I play?"

"The main victim, I think."

"So I get killed?"

"I dunno. They said it was a lead part, so I doubt it. Unless they're going for a Janet Leigh *Psycho* sort of thing."

"When can you set up a meeting?"

"They said to call them as soon as you found out, so I'll probably know later tonight."

Lizette screamed with excitement and Joey laughed along with her. They talked for a few more minutes and then he hung up so he could call the filmmakers and set everything up. Too excited to sleep, Lizette sat by her phone and watched several bad movies on television late into the night.

When her phone finally rang she was asleep on her couch and dreaming of what she would say when she won her first Oscar. Dazed, she jumped up and answered it before her machine got it.

"Joey?" she asked excitedly.

"Yeah, hi Lizette," he answered. "I talked to them and they want you to come in and meet with them today at four o'clock. Can you make it?"

"Duh!"

"Yeah, I thought so," he laughed. He then gave her the address for their office, which was in a neighborhood she had never been to before.

As soon as they hung up Lizette ran to her room and spent two hours trying to figure out what she was going to wear. It soon became clear that she had nothing that was acceptable for such an important meeting, so she ran out of her apartment and jumped into her car and drove to the nearest mall. It was there that she found the perfect outfit. It cost everything she had saved in the bank, but she knew it was worth it. She then maxed out both her credit cards on a new haircut and a manicure, so by the time she found herself driving to the meeting she was completely broke, but she looked fabulous.

Afraid that she might get lost in the strange neighborhood, she had left three hours early, because the last thing she wanted was to be late. It turned out that the office was located in a small dingy warehouse in a cold and sterile industrial park. It had actually been easy to find, so she ended up having an hour and a half to kill before the meeting. She passed the time by sitting in her parked car and reading from a book of audition monologues a former acting teacher once gave her. She also made sure to do some breathing exercises and said a few tongue twisters, so she could feel relaxed and articulate.

At four o'clock on the dot she knocked on the warehouse's front door and waited for a minute before a handsome young man in jeans and a black T-shirt opened it.

"Hi," he smiled at her, " you must be Lizette. Come on in."

Lizette smiled back at him and followed him inside.

"You look very nice today," he complimented her.

"Really?" she blushed. "It's just something I threw together."

"My name is David, and I'm the producer of this project," he said as he held out his hand for her to shake, and she shook it.

"Hi, David."

"Now why don't you follow me and we'll meet our writer-director and your costar."

"Costar? You mean I've definitely got the part?"

"Didn't Joey tell you?"

She shook her head.

"Yes, we decided that you had exactly the right look we needed for this role."

Lizette felt dizzy as she followed him to where the others were. After so many auditions where she didn't even get a thank you for coming, she had gotten her first role without even coming in.

Among the many thoughts that buzzed about in her brain, Lizette noted that the building had an odd smell she couldn't name. But she let this thought go as the two of them walked down a dusty row of shelves towards a door at the far end of the building. When they walked in she saw a short man dressed in black with a goatee and small round sunglasses and a larger, more muscular man in a plaid shirt who was sitting down and looking at his hands.

"Guys," David spoke to them, "this is Lizette. Lizette, this is our writer and director, Simon," he indicated the smaller man, "and your costar, Geoffrey."

They all shook hands and greeted each other.

Lizette was too excited to notice that the room looked nothing like any that she had seen in other production offices. The walls were a dark vibrant red and the floor was covered with plastic. She looked in the corner and saw a small digital video camera on a tripod.

"Is that for a screen test?" she pointed towards it.

"No," Simon answered, "that's the camera we're going to film with."

"Oh?" Lizette responded as she tried not to look disappointed.

"Don't worry," he laughed. "It looks dinky, but it's capable of an image almost as good as 35mm."

"Now, Lizette," David took charge, "what did Joey tell you about our film?"

"He said it was some kind of thriller."

"Sorta," he nodded his head, "but we're not really working with a script. We're going for more of a vérité-improv kind of vibe."

"Super realistic," Simon chimed in.

"Geoffrey is going to play a vicious serial killer and you're his latest victim, and what we need from you is a lot of fear and terror."

"We need you to scream."

"Do you think you can handle that?"

"Sure, I guess so," she shrugged.

"Great!" David smiled. "Let's get started!"

Simon walked over to the camera and lifted it off its tripod.

"You mean this is it?" asked Lizette. "We're not going to talk about this some more?"

"You'll be fine," answered Simon as he looked at the camera's LCD screen.

David walked over to Lizette and placed a remote microphone on her.

"Don't I need makeup?" she asked him.

"You look fine."

"Doesn't Geoffrey need a mike?"

"No, his part is silent."

A couple of minutes passed while Simon fiddled with some lights and worked out what he needed for the camera.

"All right," he said when he was finished. "Action!"

With that Geoffrey stood up and picked up something that had been beside him on the chair. It was a huge gleaming butcher knife.

"Look scared!" Simon shouted at Lizette, and she did.

Slowly Geoffrey approached her, and there was something about the way he was looking at her that unnerved her greatly. He didn't look as if he was acting. She tried to back away from him, but he grabbed her roughly and kept her from moving.

"That's great!" Simon complimented them. "Now Geoffrey, go in for the kill and Lizette scream like you've never screamed before."

Geoffrey raised his knife and Lizette howled with fear as he brought it down.

When they were finished the three men congratulated each other on another successful project.

"She was the best one so far!" Geoffrey insisted.

"Yeah," David agreed, "we'll be able to sell this one for double what we charged for the other ones."

"I don't know," Simon wondered. "She seemed a little wooden to me. It was only when the knife went in her that she seemed believable."

"You're just too picky," said David.

Simon shrugged.

"Maybe. Now do you guys want to get something to eat?"

"Yeah," said Geoffrey. "Just let me wrap up the body and dump it with the others, and we can go."

* * *

Do snuff films—as they are popularly known—really exist? Of all the questions posed by the study of urban legends, this is the one that provokes the most debate. While everyone agrees that the idea that there is an organized underground dedicated to the production and distribution of these films is ridiculous, there is some argument about whether films like this exist at all. For while there are many examples of actual deaths and murders being caught on camera by news crews, documentarians and home video enthusiasts, there are no known examples of a film of a person being killed solely so the film itself can be sold to the highest bidder.

The argument against the existence of these kinds of films is obvious. It makes no sense to make a snuff film because the film itself serves as irrefutable evidence of your crime. If it were to fall into the hands of the law and traced back to you, there would be no escape from justice. It also doesn't make sense since modern makeup and special effects techniques make it easy to fake a person's death on camera. There are, in fact, several examples of films where the producers have done exactly that. Early in the 1990s, a Japanese video named *Flower of Flesh and Blood* became infamous when well-known actor Charlie Sheen watched a copy of it and immediately contacted the FBI. The video's depiction of a young woman's murder was so realistic that the feds decided to investigate it. Their investigation ended when they got a copy of the video's sequel, which was a documentary that painstakingly showed how every violent act was faked by the filmmakers. By the end of the sequel it was clear that the smiling actress had survived the shoot without suffering a single real injury.

The argument for the existence of snuff films doesn't stand up quite as well. It depends on the belief that films like this do exist but that the people who make them and watch them are so well organized that no examples of their work ever fall into the hands of prosecutors. Like all conspiracy theories, it requires the believer to allow the conspirators a level of competence and intelligence that tends to be absent from even the most efficient organizations.

And while there have been examples of serial killers filming their victims, those films do not qualify because a) they were not made to be sold and b) none of their tapes actually show any of the murders taking place.

In 1999 this debate was refueled by the release of a Hollywood thriller, 8MM, directed by Joel Schumacher and starring Nicolas Cage. In the film Cage played a private detective hired to investigate a small, 8mm loop discovered in the safe of a recently deceased millionaire. His widow, disturbed by the violent murder depicted on the loop, hires him to find out if the film is real. His investigation leads him into a seedy L.A. underground, where he discovers the true identity of the murdered girl and avenges her death by killing the men who made the loop. The film was deliberately gritty and explicit, but the world it depicted was as much a fantasy as the story of Lizette and her sad brush with film immortality.

So do snuff films exist? Probably not. While it is theoretically possible that somewhere a film or video like that depicted in 8MM may exist, the truth is that it would be a very lonely specimen, as every other known example has been quickly proved to be a fake. There are films of people caught in their last moments, but there is no evidence that anyone has ever been killed just to make one.

The Babysitter

June had no idea what to do. It was Thanksgiving morning, and her parents and older sister were stuck at the airport. No taxi was willing to drive all the way out to Sherman's Way, despite the huge fare such a trip would bring. Normally, Craig, her husband, would pick them up, but he had been called to the hospital where he worked on an emergency and left her all alone with Sidney, their two-month-old baby.

Having not yet needed the services of a babysitter, she didn't know whom to call. Out of desperation she walked over to her neighbors' house and asked if their daughter could come over for a few hours while she picked up her family. June didn't know much about Alicia, her neighbors' 16-year-old daughter, but she assumed that like most girls her age she had no problem earning a few extra dollars babysitting. Her neighbors agreed and called Alicia to come downstairs. June felt slightly uneasy when she saw the way Alicia walked down the stairs, as she seemed unsteady and her eyes looked dazed and unfocused, but June was so desperate she didn't say anything.

Minutes later the two of them were in June's house, while June explained to Alicia how long she would be gone and what to do if Sidney woke up crying.

"Just pick him up and walk him around and pat his back," June told the teenager.

"Yeah, okay," Alicia nodded.

June was almost out the door when she realized that if the turkey was to be done in time, the babysitter would have to put it in the oven. She then spent another five minutes instructing the girl about what pan to put the turkey in, when to put it in the oven and what temperature to cook it at.

"Got it," Alicia mumbled when June was finished.

June ran out of the house and drove off to pick up her stranded family members. She was gone for two whole seconds before Alicia was on the phone with one of her friends.

"This stuff you gave me is amazing," she laughed. "I'm freaking out over here. I can, like, hear colors and stuff. I like purple the best, 'cause it sounds like sunshine."

They talked for an hour before Alicia heard the baby cry.

"Just a sec," Alicia told her friend, "I gotta check on the kid."

Alicia hung up and walked over to the baby's crib and picked him up and walked him around the house like June had told her to. By the time she got into the kitchen, he had calmed down. She was about to turn back and take him to his room when she saw on the kitchen's clock that it was time to put the turkey into the oven. She put the baby down on the kitchen counter and took out the pan and grabbed the turkey and put it all together and put it into the oven. She then grabbed the baby and took him to his room and went back to the phone and called her friend back.

"Man," she complained, "this babysitting stuff is hard."

Soon her friend had to hang up, and after that the house grew so quiet that Alicia found it difficult to stay awake. Sitting in front of the television, she drifted into a deep sleep.

She awoke with a start an hour and a half later. She looked at the clock and realized that June was going to be back right away.

"Better check on the kid," she mumbled to herself.

Thanks to her nap she was no longer as dazed as she had been when she had started babysitting that afternoon, and she was now much more able to comprehend her surroundings. Still, the sight that confronted her in the baby's crib was no easier to understand.

"Huh?" she said, scratching her head as she stared down at what she saw.

There lying in the crib was an uncooked turkey.

"I wonder where the baby is?" she said to herself as she heard June's car pull into the driveway.

* * *

If you are familiar with the above story it is probably because during the 1980s several anti-drug groups told it in their lectures and presentations as if it were true. That they would choose to prove their point with an urban legend when there would seem to be a great number of true stories that got the same point across may seem odd, but it makes sense given our natural human instinct to protect our young, an instinct that has led to many urban legends about babysitters.

Thanks to its depiction in the 1979 movie *When a Stranger Calls*, the most famous of these legends has to be the one about the young woman who is harassed by a psychotic caller who warns her about what he is going to do to her and the children she's looking after. Terrified, she calls the police who inform her that calls from the murderous stranger are coming from inside the house she's babysitting at. It is then that she goes upstairs and discovers that the kids in her charge have already been killed, and that the stranger is somewhere in the house waiting for her.

But my personal favorite is a story where the parents are much more at fault than the babysitter. In this story, which is often said to have occurred in an European country such as Norway or Holland, a couple hire a babysitter to look after their baby for a week while they go on a vacation. With just an hour to go before their plane is scheduled to leave, the babysitter has yet to arrive and the parents are getting anxious. Finally, the babysitter calls and tells them that she is caught in traffic and will be another 10 minutes. Deciding that they can't wait for her, the parents tell her that they will leave the keys she needs under their front door's welcome mat and they leave their young child in his high chair while they take off for the airport. What they don't count on is that their babysitter is killed in a car accident, so when they come home seven days later, all tanned and relaxed, they are shocked to discover the starved corpse of their baby exactly where they left him in his high chair. While there are many horrific true stories of parental neglect, it is still hard to believe that people would a) put their trip ahead of the safety of their baby and b) not call once to check up on the babysitter while they were gone.

For many parents with newborns, the idea of leaving their children with a stranger—even for just a few hours—can be very frightening, which explains why stories like these are so popular. They allow a nervous mother and/or father the excuse they need to avoid a short respite from their young child. It just goes to show that as long as there is a fear out there, there is almost always an urban legend or two to justify it.

The Initiation

Ever since the day Maurice Dudley started insisting that his friends refer to him as "Mo' Deadly" it had become clear what kind of career lifestyle he aspired to create for himself. A certified wannabe "gangsta" from the suburbs, he dreamed of hooking up with the Kaskets, the biggest and baddest gang in town. It didn't take him long to find out which bars were known Kasket meeting places, and within a couple of months he was a known fixture at these places. He developed a reputation for being a guy who told a good joke, who could be counted on to buy a few rounds and who was always one of the first guys to join in a fight. It was because of these attributes that Bullet-Bob, the leader of the Kaskets, approached him and asked him if he wanted to join his crew.

As excited as he was, Mo' knew enough to play it cool, so instead of jumping up and down like a cheerleader watching the star quarterback throw a winning touchdown, he just shrugged his shoulders and responded with a curt "what do I have to do?"

Bullet-Bob smiled.

"We got this tradition. It's an initiation we've all had to go through. Do it and you're in."

"Fine, let's do it."

"Not now," Bullet-Bob shook his head, "we've got to wait for it to be dark outside."

Mo' waited patiently for night to come as he wondered what he would have to do to become a member of the gang. Despite his willingness to join in a good bar fight, he had never done anything really illegal before. In terms of being a gangster, he was all style and no backbone. He was worried that when the moment came, he might not be able to get the job done.

Three hours later, Bullet-Bob slapped him on his back and told him that it was time to get going. He handed Mo' the keys to his truck and told him that he was going to be driving. Mo' got into the large white vehicle and asked Bullet-Bob where he was supposed to go.

"Just drive for a while," the large man answered.

Mo' started the truck and started driving down the road. For about 15 minutes the two men drove in a silence that Mo' found excruciating. Finally Bullet-Bob eased the tension by opening up the truck's glove compartment and telling Mo' what he had to do.

"It works like this," Bullet-Bob explained, "you are going to turn off your lights, and we're going to drive until someone in the other lane flashes us their high beams to let us know that our lights are off. When they do, you're going to drive them off the road, get out of the truck and shoot them with this." Bullet-Bob removed a heavy pistol from the glove compartment. "After that, you're a lifetime member. Got it?"

Mo' nodded quietly as he tried to figure out if he was capable of murdering someone in cold blood. As his conscience fought a battle inside his head, he turned off the truck's lights and drove in the darkness of the night, hoping that no one would drive by and flash their high beams at him, so that he might be spared the agony of deciding.

For 20 minutes they drove. In that time four cars passed them. Three ignored them and the fourth honked its horn. For a second, Mo' felt he was safe, but then the fifth car that they approached, a large black SUV, dashed his hopes by giving them the signal he had been dreading. In that split second he had to decide whether he would let the car drive by or run it off the road and kill whoever was inside it. Feeling he was about to throw up, he found himself turning suddenly towards the offending vehicle. The black SUV swerved to avoid crashing into him and drove into the ditch that lined the side of the road.

Mo' stopped the truck, and Bullet-Bob handed him the gun.

As quickly as he could, Mo' jumped out of the truck and ran towards the SUV. He saw that there was only one person inside it—a young woman. She looked dazed and her forehead was covered in blood, which was a result of her sudden turn into the ditch. She turned and looked at Mo' with fear and confusion in her eyes, but before she could speak he lifted up the gun in his hand and pulled the trigger three times.

"Good job, man!" Bullet-Bob congratulated him when he got back into the truck.

"Thanks," Mo' mumbled, amazed that he hadn't thrown up. "Where to now?" he asked.

"Back to the bar," Bullet-Bob answered.

Mo' turned the truck around and drove past the SUV and started to head back to where their night had begun. They were halfway there when they passed by a grocery store.

Bullet-Bob looked at his watch and swore.

"Do you think that place would still be open?"

"I dunno," Mo' answered, "probably. Why?"

"I told the old lady I'd bring home some diapers with me."

While it struck Mo' as unfathomably odd to go on a diaper run immediately after they had just killed someone, he stayed quiet and made a U-turn. There was only one other car in its parking lot, but it was clear that the store was still open, so Bullet-Bob jumped out of the truck and went in to grab some diapers. While he waited, Mo' tried not to think about what he had done. He tried not to imagine the look on the young woman's face as he pulled the trigger. He tried not to picture what her family looked like and how they would react to the news that she had been murdered. He tried not to wonder if she was married and if she had any children. He was so busy trying not to do any of these things that he barely noticed the cry of pain that echoed through the night air. He glanced out of his truck's windshield and was surprised to see Bullet-Bob lying on the parking lot's pavement. He was grabbing his ankle, from which crimson splatters of blood were spraying out as if he was a fountain.

Mo' jumped out of the truck and saw a darkly dressed figure jump up from under the other car in the parking lot. He ran into the car and started to drive away. Mo' lifted his gun and shot at the fleeing man, but he was too far away and too lousy a shot to hit him. He ran to Bullet-Bob, who was screaming in pain.

"What happened?" asked Mo' as he tried to stop the bleeding with his hands.

"Demons," Bullet-Bob hissed, referring to the town's other gang. "They make their initiates hide under cars and slash people's ankles," he explained before using a long string of curse words to describe how he felt about the practice.

"I'll call 911," Mo' told him. He started to run towards the store, but Bullet-Bob yelled at him to stop.

"Don't call 911, they'll get the cops involved. Go to that payphone over there and call the bar and ask for Doc Rock. He'll know what to do."

Mo' nodded and turned and ran towards the payphone that stood beside the grocery store. He lifted the phone from the cradle and threw some coins into the slot. He dialed the number to the bar, but before anyone could answer he started to feel woozy. The tips of his fingers were burning and the phone dropped out of his hands as he slumped to the ground.

For a few seconds a voice on the other end of the phone waited for him to answer, but Mo' couldn't speak. By the time the person hung up, Mo' was dead.

Bullet-Bob was close to passing out as the blood continued to spurt out of him. He had just enough strength to look up and see Mo' slumped down in the payphone. As he began to fade, he remembered listening to Fat Freddie and Za-Blade earlier that night. They had been bragging about how they had gone around town and spread a potentially fatal combination of strychnine and LSD on the buttons of random payphones.

He had laughed when he had heard them talk about it, but now, as he was just minutes from bleeding to death, he didn't think it was so funny.

* * *

In the world of urban legends, gangs are frequently used as all-purpose bogeymen. Striking randomly and without explanation, they are always described as ruthless predators who attack without the slightest provocation. Just who these gang members are and why they do what they do is seldom explained. The answer, it would seem, is simply because they are evil and take great pleasure in killing the innocent.

It would be foolish to deny that gangs like the Kaskets and the Demons exist, but it would be equally foolish to live in fear of the activities ascribed to them in the above conglomeration of three well-known legends. The truth is that as cruel and vicious as real gangs can be, they perform their criminal activities to make money, not to kill random civilians. The leaders of these gangs—most famously embodied by such groups as the Krips, the Bloods and the Hell's Angels—are savvy enough to realize that if their members were to go about and kill people for fun, the result would be an even harder police crackdown than they already face, a crackdown that would not be good for business. While there are many cases of innocent people being caught in the middle of a gang war, the reality remains that a gang member is much more likely to kill another gang member than a person buying groceries.

As hard as it may be for some people to accept, no one has ever been killed for flashing their high beams. There is no evidence that a gang has ever required its members to slash at people's ankles in parking lots, and there has yet to be a single death that has been directly attributed to poison being painted onto a payphone's buttons. So, while a person should always be vigilant about their surroundings, these are three potential occurrences you really have no reason to worry about.

Her Loyal Protector

Carrie's parents were standing at the door and about to leave. She couldn't get over how different they looked. Her mother was the definition of elegance in her sleek cocktail dress, and her father looked like a 1940s' film star in his suit. As good as they looked, though, there was still an air of discomfort in their bearing. This was the first time they were going to leave Carrie alone in the house at night without a babysitter. When they had first heard about the party they were all set to get her one, but Carrie reminded them that she was only a few weeks away from her 13th birthday and was almost as old as some of the sitters they had hired for her in the past. They knew she was right, but they weren't happy about it.

"Do you have the number to the Sarrazens?" her mother asked.

"Yes," Carrie sighed, "it's right by the phone, where you left it."

"What do you do if a stranger comes into the house?" asked her father, who had been teaching her different crime-prevention strategies all week.

"Run out of the house and go next door to Mrs. Spangler's house," she answered.

"And?"

"Call 911," she added. "Shouldn't you guys be going? You're going to be late."

Her mother and father looked at each other with mutual expressions of uncertainty.

"Don't worry," Carrie rolled her eyes with exasperation, "even if something does happen, I've got Jeremy to look after me. Don't I, Jeremy?"

Hearing his name caused the family's German shepherd to perk up his ears and sit up. He panted happily as Carrie walked over to him and gave him a scratch behind his ears. Seeing this actually helped to ease her parents' fears. While they knew how gentle their big dog was, they also knew that he looked imposing enough to frighten off even the most courageous criminals. They quizzed her one more time about all the relevant phone numbers and emergency drills before they finally left for the party.

Free at last, Carrie waited until their car was out of sight before she started doing all the things that were normally forbidden. She turned up the stereo to an ear-shattering volume, called a bunch of her friends and watched a movie on one of the channels her parents tried to block. As exciting as all this was, she still couldn't fight the inevitable sleepiness that started to creep over her. She made a valiant effort to stay up past her bedtime but was asleep on the couch five minutes later. She slept there for half an hour before she woke up again and got up to go and sleep in her bed. Jeremy followed her into her bedroom and slumped down beside her bed. She changed into her pajamas and got into bed. As she lay there she held her left hand off the edge and giggled while Jeremy tickled her by licking it. Five minutes later she was asleep once again. The hours began to pass.

Though she was not prone to nightmares, Carrie's sleep was disturbed by a far-off dripping sound, like that from a leaky faucet. She tried to ignore it, but as it continued it grew more and more irritating. Looking for something to relax her, she once again put her left hand over the edge of her bed. Jeremy obliged her by licking it as he had done before. This comforted her and helped her to ignore the dripping sound and within minutes she was in such a deep sleep she wouldn't have heard the roar of Niagara Falls if she was in a barrel going down it.

Morning came and she awoke with a long yawn. She hoped her parents were up already because she wanted to quiz them about the party and let them know how she had survived the night without a hitch. She decided to change out of her pajamas first and opened up her closet.

Her parents, who had still been asleep, were awoken by the loudest and longest scream of terror either of them had ever heard. They both jumped out of bed and ran to Carrie's room where they found her huddled in a corner, shaking and crying. Before they could ask what was wrong, Carrie's mom turned towards the closet and let loose with a scream as powerful as her daughter's.

There they saw Jeremy hanging from a rope. His neck had been cut and the carpet on the closet's floor was covered with slowly drying blood. Pinned on his chest was a sheet of paper on which a note was written in purple crayon. It read, "Dogs aren't the only ones who can lick things, you know."

* * *

It makes sense that since there are so many legends about the bad things that can happen when you hire a babysitter, there would have to also be some legends about the dangers of not hiring one. What makes this story different from its opposites is that it has no real identifiable moral. Unlike the stoned babysitter or the baby in the high chair, there doesn't seem to be much of a lesson to learn here. The problem is that the crime committed in the story is so completely unmotivated. There is no explanation as to why the dog was killed and why the killer was so keen to keep Carrie in bed by licking her fingers. It seems more like a horribly ghoulish practical joke than a violent crime.

What makes this story more disturbing than it really deserves is the age of the protagonist. If the story was about a woman 10 years older, it would make for a macabre but humorous tale, but with a 12-year-old girl as the victim the effect is much more disturbing. But having a younger protagonist distracts from the story's faults, of which there are too many to count. Legends like this take years, if not decades, to develop, during which time they are carefully refined to allow for maximum impact. Chances are that this story did develop as a dark joke, but that after years of fine-tuning it was transformed into a disturbing cautionary tale. What that caution may be, though, is a subject open to a really silly debate.

6

You're not Going to Believe This, But...

A ssuming that you aren't sneakily skipping ahead and reading this last chapter first, then it is safe to assume that you have—over the course of the previous five chapters—developed a nose for the scent of an urban legend. Now that you've seen 40 different legends debunked before your very eyes, you're equipped with a healthy skepticism you can now use whenever you hear a story that sounds just too good or too wild to be true. You're now something of an expert on the subject and can no longer be fooled. Or so you thought.

The following eight stories are presented to show you that the world of urban legends isn't as cut and dried as you may think. At first glance all these stories are as outlandish and unlikely as the 40 legends that have preceded them, but looks can be deceiving. Despite their strong resemblance to urban lore, they are all stories of things that really happened. They serve as proof that the fact that a story sounds too incredible to be believed doesn't mean it didn't really happen.

They Never Saw
These Two Coming

Strange deaths are such a large part of urban legend lore there's a whole chapter dedicated to them in this book (see Chapter Four: A Strange Way to Go). The two stories about to be described here could easily be included among those tales of bizarre fatalities, if it were not for one key difference— they both really happened. As hard as it is to believe, these two similar tales of man-made disaster are members of that rare creature, the urban legend that turns out to be true. And both are prime examples of the belief that when it's your time to go, the universe will find a way to get you, no matter how incredible it may be.

The first incident occurred in St. Giles, a quiet London neighborhood, on October 17, 1814. The citizens of this community had gone about their daily routine without a clue that one of the most bizarre disasters of all time was about to befall them. It all began in a local brewery when a huge vat of beer ruptured suddenly and without explanation. Over 3500 gallons of the pale brew sprayed out in a torrent and escaped from the building and swept through the streets. The wave of beer was so large and powerful it swept people off their feet and destroyed two houses.

In the 1983 cult movie *Strange Brew*, there is a scene where the quintessential hoser and beer-fanatic Bob McKenzie, as played by Rick Moranis, finds himself trapped inside a large vat that is slowly filling up with beer. As the amber liquid rises higher and higher, he admits to the woman trapped with him that he used to dream about being in this situation, but now that it was really happening to him, "it bites." One can only assume that this was the sentiment felt by all those who were hit by the flood of beer that fateful day in London. If you were to ask any of them how they would feel if they were given gallons and gallons of free lager, they would say "great!"—until they were informed they may die in the process.

For 105 years, London's infamous beer flood was easily the most incredible event of its kind, but in 1919 a similar disaster in Boston stole the title away with a flood that was as agonizingly slow as it was deadly. The date was January 15, and the weather was unseasonably warm. It was 46° F that day, which was just warm enough to cause an enormous tank filled with 2,320,000 gallons of molasses to explode. The result was a 30-foot-tall tidal wave of the heavy black syrup that was so powerful it crushed buildings and threw all that lay in its path up into the air. People drowned and were crushed by the goo, the stickiness of which made the situation even worse, as rescuers became mired in the 14,000 tons of it that covered the ground. In the end 21 people were killed and 150 were seriously injured. It took years for the city's north end to recover from the ensuing damage, and to this day people still insist that you can smell molasses in the air on warm summer days.

Chances are if you were to try to tell someone that people actually died in floods of beer and molasses, they would laugh you off as either some kind of fool or practical joker, but the truth is that sometimes things happen that are so absurd they defy all our notions of reality. Whereas so many stories in this book sound like they could happen, even though they are completely illogical, these two stories sound unlikely, but there is nothing about them that doesn't make any sense. Both beer and molasses can be stored in large vats, which are capable of accidentally bursting open, and people can die if these substances hit them with enough force. It is only the likelihood of these events occurring that strains credulity, which proves people are often more willing to believe illogical stories that sound like they could happen every day over logical stories that may happen only once in all of human history.

For His Efforts in Population Control

Around the time that Texas governor George W. Bush was running for president of the United States in 1999 an urban legend began to spread that the man whose state led the country in annual state-sanctioned executions had allowed a resolution to pass in his legislature that honored a notorious serial killer. The subtext of the legend was that it wasn't hard to believe that a state government capable of making such an obvious faux pas was equally capable of executing an innocent man. This politically motivated legend was—in essence— based on fact, but the timeline had been shifted so that the story could be used against Bush. The truth was that the Texas legislature had passed a resolution that honored a serial killer, but it had done so 28 years earlier in 1971, long before Bush held the office of governor.

At that time Rep. Tom Moore, Jr., from Waco had become frustrated by his peers' practice of rubber-stamping resolutions without reading them or even knowing what they were about. Given the large volume of such measures that were placed in front of each official, it was essentially impossible to read each one, so it was considered professional courtesy to just sign the resolution with the understanding that fellow representatives wouldn't include anything in it that could be embarrassing. Rep. Moore decided that he was going to break this practice by sponsoring a resolution that honored a man named Albert De Salvo.

To the public at large De Salvo was better known as the Boston Strangler, who had been accused of murdering 13 women between 1962 and 1964. In 1971 he was serving a life sentence for sexual assault (he had never actually been tried or convicted for the murders) when Rep. Moore drafted a resolution thanking him for his "dedication and devotion to his work [which] has enabled the weak and the lonely throughout the nation to achieve and maintain a new degree of concern for their future." The resolution also pointed out that "[De Salvo has] been officially recognized by the state of Massachusetts for his noted activities and unconventional techniques involving population control and applied psychology."

Just as Rep. Moore had expected, this resolution passed unanimously without a comment. It was only then that he withdrew the resolution and chastened his peers for what they had done. They were understandably embarrassed and angered by his sneaky trick, but the reality of their workload still made it impossible for them to change their ways, so the practice of rubber-stamping similar documents continued.

There is no record of De Salvo's reaction to his being honored (if he even heard about it). He had little time to appreciate it anyway, as a fellow prisoner stabbed him to death in 1973. To this day he remains a controversial figure because he was never charged or tried for the murders he confessed to, leading some to theorize that he wasn't responsible for the murders and that the real Boston Strangler was allowed to remain free. Such a theory is, however, pure speculation, and most people are satisfied that the man who was honored by the state of Texas in 1971 for his "activities…involving population control" was the man who had terrorized the women of Boston for those two harrowing years.

No Plate

Of all the annoyances that people face as they move through traffic, perhaps the most irritating is coming across one of those vanity license plates. While some of them are simple and straightforward, the majority—which attempt the near impossible task of describing someone's personality in seven letters and/or numbers—are utterly incomprehensible. And so, along with all the other distractions that can plague a driver, people often find themselves using their last bit of mental space trying to decipher some meaning from messages like DTH8MOI or BLDNSXY, while the owners of these plates drive by, blissfully unaware of the strain they are putting on their fellow motorists. It is because of this that there is much pleasure to be had in the discovery that the following story, which has existed as an urban legend for two decades now, is 100 percent true. It is somehow satisfying to know that at some point a carelessly chosen plate cost its driver thousands of dollars in traffic tickets.

In 1979 a Los Angeles resident named Robert applied for a vanity plate. An avid boatman, Robert had wanted a plate that proved to the world his passion for the sea. So he put down SAILING and BOATING as his choices for plates on his application form. The form requested that he make a third choice, in case his first two were unavailable, but Robert couldn't think of another one he liked, so he wrote down "no plate." He had meant that he didn't want a plate if SAILING and BOATING were taken—which, of course, they had been long before—but the person responsible for handling the forms either took him literally or decided to have some fun with him. A few weeks later Robert received his new plate in the mail and to his shock it read NO PLATE.

As disappointed as he was, Robert decided that correcting the mistake wasn't worth the time it would take, so he decided to just use the plate. At least, he figured, there was something a little surreal and unique about a license plate that denied its own existence. What he didn't know was that computers cannot comprehend the surreal and it didn't take long for his new plate to get him into trouble with the law.

At that time whenever a police officer in California wrote a parking ticket for a car that had no visible license plate they would write "no plate" in the space where the license number would usually go. Before Robert got his new plates, the DMV computers would just skip over that part of the ticket, but now they had a specific car with the license number of NO PLATE and as a result he was sent every single citation that otherwise would have not been sent to anyone. Over the course of a few months he was sent over 2500 traffic tickets from all over the state. He immediately contacted the DMV, and workers there suggested he change his plate, even though it was their fault that he had it in the first place. By then Robert had grown to like his special plate and wanted to keep it, so he started mailing the tickets back along with a form letter that explained the situation. This usually worked, but more than once he had to go to court to prove his case to a judge.

The situation lasted for several years until finally the DMV sent out a message to the police, requesting that they instead write "none" or "missing" on their tickets, instead of "no plate." For Robert this proved to be the solution to his problem, but it caused headaches for a man whose license plate was—you guessed it—MISSING.

How Scary Is It Now?

While some are better than others, the "spooky" funhouse is almost always the lamest attraction at any carnival. Perhaps this is why it's also the one that carnival organizers work the hardest to get you into. The paintings on its outside, with their depictions of scary vampires, snarling werewolves and lumbering Frankenstein's monsters, lure you into thinking that the inside of the building is a virtual nonstop cavalcade of thrills and adventure. Plus a huckster often stands outside and tells passersby about the kind of exciting adventures they are missing by walking past him and heading towards the Ferris wheel.

But the truth is that once you're inside, you have to settle for canned "scary" music, phony-looking plastic monsters, some cobwebs and—if you're very lucky—a guy in a mask earning minimum wage jumping out at you near the end. While this may prove terrifying for very small children or the claustrophobic, the majority of people have scarier times trying to get home during rush hour. Perhaps this is one reason there are several urban legends about funhouses and what they really contain. If a group of kids know how boring the ride is, they might still be able to be tricked into going into it if they've heard that the guy who jumps out at you at the end is really the freakishly deformed son of the carnival's owner, who doesn't allow his monstrous child out in the daylight for fear of his being mobbed by a cruel and frightened public. One of the most popular of these funhouse legends is the one that insists that the dummy hanging from the noose in the corner is really the corpse of a famous outlaw, but unlike the other legends, this one—just once—had the distinction of being true.

In the last month of 1976, the producers of the hit Lee Majors' action television show *The Six Million Dollar Man* decided to film a segment of one of their episodes inside an old funhouse located at the Nu-Pike Amusement Park in Long Beach, California. As the crew worked to get equipment set up and start filming, a production assistant was asked to move the funhouse's hanging dummy because it looked too phony for the director's liking. The P.A. grabbed it by its arm to pull it down, but instead the arm just came off and the body began to swing back and forth. As the P.A. held the arm in his hands, it was obvious that it didn't feel like anything a dummy might be made of. He looked at where it had ripped off and was shocked to discover what looked like bone. The arm in his hands was a real arm, and the dummy swinging behind him was a genuine corpse.

As it turned out, the dead man had had quite a career on the carnival circuit. His name was Elmer McCurdy. He wasn't a very bright fellow, and his only option for finding fame and fortune was to become an outlaw, but he wasn't any good at it. In 1911 he decided to rob a train, an extremely dangerous way to make some money. For his efforts he netted $46 and two bottles of whiskey, which even back then was a pathetically paltry amount. But even though his take was minimal, train robbing was considered a very serious offence and a posse was rounded up to catch him. It didn't take long for them to back him into a corner, but instead of surrendering he shouted out those clichéd last words "you'll never take me alive!" And they didn't. Elmer died in a hail of gunfire.

Normally the story of a person's life would end with his or her death, but in Elmer's case, his death was just the beginning. After he was killed his corpse was taken to a local mortuary, where he was embalmed in preparation for his burial. But before he was laid to rest, the undertaker took a look at the outlaw—whose body was unclaimed—and decided he had never seen a corpse look so good. It was partly out of pride for his excellent work and partly out of a desire to make a few extra dollars that the undertaker decided to dress Elmer's corpse in some fancy clothes and prop him in a corner in his back room. It was there that he billed him as "The Bandit Who Wouldn't Give Up." Curious townsfolk went to check this curiosity out and paid by slipping a nickel into Elmer's open mouth. This was how his career in show business began.

Elmer sat there for four years before two enterprising businessmen sensed a good opportunity and forged some documents to indicate that they were related to Elmer. With these they were to take him from the undertaker and tour him around the South at carnivals, sideshows and any place else a quick buck could be made. He even appeared in a few low-budget films before he finally ended up at the funhouse in Long Beach. He hung there for so long that people forgot where he had come from and didn't know that he had once been a real person. That was why no one warned the crew of the TV show that they would have to deal with the dead if they wanted to film there.

After the TV crew discovered him he was taken down and given a proper burial in 1977. Afraid that his notoriety might cause him to become abducted by some ambitious grave robbers, the state ensured that he would stay under the ground by pouring 2 feet of concrete over his casket. He's been there ever since, having earned his retirement.

Edison's Unintentional Invention

Few men have had as profound an impact on the world as Thomas Edison, the inventor who held 1093 patents before he died in 1931. For example, if you are reading this in a room illuminated by a light bulb, then you are feeling the effects of his work. Along with artificial light, he also gave us the phonograph, which allowed people—for the first time—to listen to prerecorded music and speeches, and the kinetoscope, one of the first methods for watching moving images. But what earned him the nickname "The Wizard of Menlo Park" wasn't so much his genius at invention as his genius for self-promotion. The truth is that men who worked for Edison invented many of the items for which patents were listed under his name, but thanks to his reputation it was nearly impossible to convince the public that he wasn't 100 percent responsible for each of his inventions. In addition to this talent for self-promotion Edison had the heart of a ruthless businessman. Edison wasn't above employing the occasional underhanded trick to discredit rivals or put them out of business completely.

According to a popular legend about Edison, it was this willingness to aim straight for his opponents' gut that led to the invention of the electric chair. And even though Edison was opposed to capital punishment, this legend—as it turns out—is completely historically accurate. The electric chair was invented because Edison supported a less-efficient energy delivery system.

As the man who had invented the light bulb, Edison had a serious interest in bringing electricity to all the cities he could. As preferable as they were to gas lamps, light bulbs worked only if a house was equipped with the energy to turn them on. To solve this dilemma, he developed a system that ran on direct current, which—based mainly on the faith inspired by his name—he was able to sell to downtown New York City. The problem was that Edison's system was highly impractical. Direct current is capable of traveling only a few city blocks, and it requires nearly every home to own a large and noisy generator. While this was acceptable for small, enclosed areas, it made no sense for rapidly growing cities.

Sensing an opening in the market, another inventor named George Westinghouse, who had previously made a fortune inventing an air brake for trains, developed a system that employed alternating current to send energy into homes. This system allowed cities to build just a few generators, which could be built in remote areas, or even out of town, as alternating current was capable of traveling much farther than direct current. Trying to find an angle with which to fight this obviously superior product, Edison chose to focus on the fact that alternating current was potentially much more dangerous than his direct alternative. He waged a fear campaign against his competitor and tried to make alternating current illegal. He printed pamphlets warning of the apocalypse that could arise if Westinghouse's system was used, and he decided to show reporters just how dangerous it could be.

With the press present, one of his aides—a man named H.P. Brown—proved that alternating current could be lethal by using it on stray animals, which he bought from local children for a quarter a piece. Suitably horrified for Edison's liking, the journalists wrote graphic accounts of what they saw. One of these accounts landed on the lap of then-governor of New York, David B. Hill. Hill had set up a commission devoted to finding more humane methods with which to execute criminal offenders. At that time criminals were hanged for their crimes, and reports of men being slowly asphyxiated because the nooses were too loose or being decapitated because the nooses were too tight had caused enough of a public outcry for the state to start searching for a more effective method. Reading about what Brown had done to animals piqued the governor's interest, and he asked the commission to ask Edison about the possibility of using the same method on criminals.

At first Edison refused to talk to the commission, as he was opposed to all forms of capital punishment, but then he realized that the state might have given him the perfect opportunity to discredit his rival. He sent a telegraph to the commission that recommended "electricide" as the most humane way possible to execute someone, but he did not stop there. He went on to suggest that the best generators with which to kill a person were "alternating machines, manufactured principally in this country by George Westinghouse."

Thanks to Edison, the New York legislature passed a bill adopting the electric chair as its official method of execution. The first person to feel the effects of this decision was a murderer named William Kemmler. Kemmler's lawyer tried to stop the electrocution by arguing that it amounted to cruel and unusual punishment, but—thanks to testimony from Edison in which he insisted that the prisoner would not suffer—the judge ruled against him. Kemmler was executed on August 6, 1890, and opinions about the method's success were definitely mixed. The *New York Times* insisted that Kemmler appeared to suffer much more than if he had been hanged, while the commissioner who had supported the new method thought it was "the grandest success of the age."

Unfortunately for Edison, his trickery didn't work. Kemmler's execution did not lead to a public outcry about the dangers of alternating current, and Westinghouse's more efficient system was adopted throughout the country. And even though it had never been meant to be anything more than a publicity tool, electrocution became a popular form of execution throughout the United States.

If They Found Him,
They Can Find You

In the United States, young men are required to register for
the draft within a month after their 18th birthday. Failure to
do so can result in a fine as high as $250,000 and/or up to
five years in prison, but even such serious threats of punishment aren't enough to get everyone who is eligible to sign up.
Whether it's because of a philosophical opposition to serving
in the military, fear of being killed in combat or ignorance
about the law, there are thousands of men within the age
restrictions of 18 to 26 who have never registered. Part of the
Selective Service System's job is to find these men and get
them to sign up or alert the authorities about their criminal
noncompliance. So diligent is this government agency in its
duties, a legend is often told about how they have even sent
out reminders to men who never existed, and by now you've
figured out that if it's being told in this chapter, then the
legend must be true. It is.

In 1984 Johnny Klomberg, whose address was listed as in
the town of Palo Alto, California, received a letter from the
draft board that informed him that he was coming close to
turning 18 and that he would be required to register. But
Johnny wasn't turning 18 that year, nor did he live at the
address listed on the envelope. He had never lived there, as he
was the fictitious creation of two young boys looking to get
some free ice cream.

Brothers Greg and Eric Hentzel had discovered a clever
way to scam free sundaes from a chain restaurant called
Farrell's Ice Cream Parlour. The restaurant offered free ice

cream to kids on their birthdays, and all they had to do to get it was fill out a form that asked for their name, address and date of birth. They would then get a coupon for their free sundae within a week of their birthday. The Hentzel boys were smart enough to figure out that all they had to do was fill out a bunch of the forms with different names and birth dates but with the same address, and they would receive a coupon more than once a year. Johnny Klomberg was just one of the many imaginary aliases they created to satisfy their sweet tooth.

What the boys did not know was that the restaurant occasionally rented its mailing list to other companies through a direct mail broker. In cases such as this, companies are allowed to approve whom the broker gives their list to, so that—for example—a list of children's names isn't given to a lingerie company. But what Farrell's did not know was that their broker went behind their back and sold their list of 167,000 names to the Selective Service System for $5687. With it, the draft board was able to make a list of all the boys who were close to turning 18, and they sent reminders to them that they had only a few months to register. As it turned out, Johnny Klomberg was included in that list, and he received his notice just like the others, even though he had never existed.

The Killer Golf Tee

Among aficionados of the golfing world, there is an oft-told legend about the duffer who had the habit of chewing on his golf tees when he was playing a bad round. He believed that chewing the little wooden pegs helped him concentrate and kept his mind off his slices and missed putts, but he was unaware of a potentially fatal consequence of his habit. According to the legend, the golfer spent three horrible rounds chewing on a tee that—unlike the others he usually chewed on—had actually been used in the ground, and what he did not know was that the tee had become covered with the pesticides the grounds crew used to keep insects from eating the grass. As he chewed on the tee, the poisons from the pesticides got into his system, and just as he made his putt on the 18th hole, he dropped dead from toxic shock.

As strange as this may sound, this story is really true, although several of the details have been changed to make it more dramatic. It all happened at the Army-Navy Country Club in Arlington, Virginia, where in 1982, after three rounds of golf, a 30-year-old Navy Lieutenant named George M. Prior complained to his friends that he had a headache. When he went home, his migraine got worse and he became nauseated, developed a fever and became covered in an ugly, burning rash. Within 10 days he was dead. While he suffered from a 104.5° fever, his rash grew and blistered, until it covered 80 percent of his body. At that point his organs began to fail.

The cause of this lieutenant's early death was determined to have been exposure to Daconil, a fungicide. The grounds crew at the country club sprayed the chemical on the course twice a week and had sprayed it the day George had played

those three rounds. The tee he chewed on had been exposed to the chemical, and it ended up causing a fatal allergic reaction.

While many people describe golf as a boring sport, this story serves as proof that along with all those other tales of golfers killed by flying golf balls, bolts of lightning or heart attacks caused by enraged reactions to badly executed swings, it is—in its own way—a dangerous and extreme sport.

The Baby Derby

There are many legends and stories about contests between men, many of which become important parts of American folklore. One good example is the story of John Henry, the black man who was the greatest railroad builder of all time. Able to hammer down more spikes in 10 minutes than 10 ordinary men could in an hour, John found himself pitted in a contest against a machine built by the railroad to do his job. If he won the contest, he and his friends would get to keep the job, and if he lost, the machine would take their place. As hard as John fought, his body was no match for the unstoppable stamina of the machine, and his heart exploded before the contest was over. There are many other legends similar to this one, and they all have one thing in common— they are all battles fought by men. Women are almost never in these legends, except maybe as a reason for why the contest is being waged. This is what makes the story of the baby derby so unique, as it is about a contest that could be fought only by women. The other aspect of the legend that makes it unique is that it really happened. Over 75 years ago there really was a contest to see which woman could give birth to the most children within a 10-year span.

The contest was the result of the perverse sense of humor of a Toronto lawyer named Charles Vance Millar. A lifelong bachelor, Charles had made a fortune taking the kind of business gambles that most sensible investors avoided. The ease with which he made his money allowed him to see the silliness of it all. He loved exploring the way money made people act, how it made them so easily abandon their principles. He used to deliberately drop dollar bills on sidewalks just so he could watch the expression of people's faces as they picked them up and pocketed them. And when he drafted his will, he decided to have some fun.

Three of his beneficiaries were given valuable shares in the Ontario Jockey Club. The first man was a known crook whose past would never have allowed him membership into the club, and the other two were men who had campaigned against the ill-effects of racetrack betting. These last two men were put in the quandary of either cashing in on their good fortune or refusing it out of principle, while the elitist club had to deal with a shareholder who did not meet its exclusive standards. As well, one share of another jockey club was given to every minister in three nearby towns. The agony they spent trying to decide what to do with their inheritances was proved unwarranted when they discovered the shares were worth less than a penny.

Similar bequests in his will were just as cruel, but the one that captured the public's imagination when Millar died in 1926 at the age of 73 was his will's ninth clause. It read as follows:

All the rest and residue of my property wheresoever situate I give, devise and bequeath unto my Executors and Trustees named below in Trust to convert into money as they deem advisable and invest all the money until the expiration of nine years from my death and then call in and convert it all into money and at the expiration of ten years from my death to give it and its accumulations to the Mother who has since my death given birth in Toronto to the greatest number of children as shown by the Registrations under the Vital Statistics Act. If one or more mothers have equal highest number of registrations

under the said Act to divide the said moneys and accumula-
tions equally between them.

For those of you out there uncomfortable with the verbal tricks of legalese, what this says simply is that the woman in Toronto who gave birth to the most babies between the day of Charles' death and its 10-year anniversary would receive whatever remained of his estate. At the time of his death he had been worth $100,000, but thanks to one of his riskier investments this total jumped to $750, 000, which—as the Great Depression took hold of North America—was enough to cause a near riot. As scores of Toronto women began to deliberately get pregnant in hopes of winning, the will was taken to court several times to answer questions about the clause's legality and possible danger to the pub-lic. As well, the courts were asked to decide what the will meant by Toronto (did it include the city's many suburbs?) and about the eligibility of stillborn and illegitimate chil-dren. Charles' distant relatives also went to court to have the will invalidated.

By the time all the legal wrangling was over (the matter was eventually decided in the Supreme Court of Canada) the 10 years stipulated had already passed. The court had allowed Charles' clause to stand, and four women tied for the win. Annie Smith, Kathleen Nagle, Isabel MacLean and Lucy Timleck each received $125,000 for having each had nine chil-dren within the 10-year period. Two other women were rewarded $12,500 each. Both Pauline Clarke and Lillian Kerry had had 10 children during that time, but Pauline was disqual-ified because some of her children were illegitimate, and Lillian was disqualified because two of her children were stillborn.

As much as Charles enjoyed a good prank at the expense of people's greed, it's hard to believe that he knew his clause would have such an impact on people. While there is no record of how many children were born as the result of the derby, it's easy to imagine that whole families were built on the desire to get a piece of his fortune. Hundreds, possibly thousands, of people are alive today because of a single paragraph in a long will, and if that isn't the stuff of legends, what is?

The End